10-1

My 10-Year Journey from Suicide Attempt to Ultramarathon Runner

Laura Bird

Contents

Dedication

For my 'Ray' of sunshine. Thank you for teaching me, showing me and inspiring me with the happy realisation of just how beautiful life is.

For Amanda. Thank you for being on the other side of every single finish line I cross. Thank you for showing dedication beyond measure. I love you.

For every single person who has ever doubted whether they are enough. Yes, you are.

Prologue

There was very little to be seen in the clinical side room of Addenbrooke's Hospital that had been imprisoning me for nearly three and a half weeks. There were no Get Well Soon cards being gradually faded by the winter sunshine, sitting by the tiny crack of light seeping through the box window. There was no half-eaten basket of grapes nestled into a selection of trashy women's magazines, detailing how Doris, the 58-year-old dinner lady, had 7 children by 10 different men (and is still trying to work out which one belongs to whom) but was also respectfully making the decision to now live her life as Daniel and was setting up a 'Go Fund Me' page for the much-needed surgery. There was no warmth or comfort in my temporary bedroom that was providing as much privacy as a peephole. Any scrap of time to myself I may have got was soon violated by the next nurse, doctor or mental health worker coming along to prod, probe or pry. My body was a patchwork quilt of intricate sterilised dressings and bandages healing the gaping wounds they were trying to cover. Beneath the external patchwork quilt was a camouflage of black and blue bruising, covering 80% of the peach skin that was being totally overwhelmed by its dark, navy evil sister. It was as though I'd been invited to a Smurf fancy dress party the night before. I looked as if I'd covered myself in deep blue paint, had a few Sherbets, got a bit sweaty then woken the next morning (inevitably not in my own bed) to find patchy dark blue expanses smudged in every orifice you can envisage. Somewhere within this bizarre Smurf party, Papa Smurf had managed to construct some sturdy internal metalwork inside my right thigh, to piece together some of my shattered frame. I was imprisoned in so many different ways; not just because I was keeping deathly still, in my totally bed-bound condition, so as not to irritate any one of the list of horrific injuries that I had sustained, but also because I'd tried so desperately hard to end the psychological trauma that haunted me every day, which also landed me in this predicament, to then only have to awake every morning and face it all once more.

I really wasn't justified in having any complaints. I wasn't restricted to this rather awful Air B 'n' B because I had tragically come down with a life-threatening disease or heroically saved a puppy from a house fire. And I certainly wasn't recovering from a garish blue fancy dress party that a few Alka-Seltzers and a fry up could fix. I had single-handedly placed myself here. The lack of sympathy cards, Take A Break magazines and extortionate grapes from the food court shops was, I think, because of a bout of confusion amongst my peers and loved ones, an hour and a half down the road back in Ipswich, as to how exactly I ended up there. There was genuine concern matched with a definite ambiguity as to why I had gone from bouncing around the Sixth Form College corridors on a Friday afternoon, to being unconscious, lying in Intensive Care, the following Monday. That is one heavy weekend whichever way you look at it. You see, I was a master of deception when it came to projecting what I was genuinely feeling. There would have not been one friend, colleague, teacher or completely random stranger who I came into contact with on that Friday 12th November 2010, who would have suggested there was even anything mildly wrong, let alone allow it to be conceivable that just hours after the school day had finished, four days after turning the ripe old age of 18, I would be attempting to commit suicide in one of the most graphic ways imaginable.

The story that began circulating the same corridors I had been prancing around just days earlier was that I'd been involved in a severe car accident and needed to be hospitalised for a number of weeks. I can just imagine the troubled thought process of the handful of individuals *actually* in the know as to what really happened.

'Can we really tell them she has done that? They are going to notice she isn't around; what are we going to say? Is she awake yet, can we ask her? Can we let people see her? Mocks are just around the corner; this could be really damaging to the other students.'

The trouble with the car accident saga (road traffic collision if we are being technical) was my beloved KA at the time didn't have a scratch on it. Yes, it had the rust buckets and wear and tear of any proud first car, but not enough to convince 300-odd adolescents it had been involved in a major smash. At the time, I didn't invest any effort in conducting reviews of the local body shop repair services; but I'm quite sure the near-destroyed physical state of my body did not match the pristine state of my car. I'm sure I'd have received some funny looks asking to pay for my car to be damaged to validate a fabricated story. Even if a few panels could be beaten about a bit, I'm just not sure the car accident story was going to cut it. Even if poor little Lilly the KA sustained £200 worth of damage, that was probably 50 quid more than she was worth anyway. It should have been written off if as much as a windscreen wiper went missing.

The next addition to the bemusement of my peers was that the buoyant, outgoing and extrovert personality that I was known for, definitely did not match the characteristics of that same young woman stood alone, shivering in a lay by, seconds away from trying to take her own life. The rumour mill would be working overtime and the levels of concern and confusion amongst a bustling Sixth Form College community would be rife. I suppose, however, addressing an impressionable and pre-occupied collection of 18-year-olds and telling them their friend was fighting for her life in hospital after walking straight out in front of an articulated lorry, travelling at 60 miles per hour on the A14 dual carriageway in an attempt to kill herself, was a hugely unenviable task, for even the most experienced of educators.

The long, lonely painful days sat in that room would have been gratefully interrupted by a string of familiar faces, but other than the closest of friends and family, no one else came to see the mess I was in. I was evidently being protected by those closest to me when it was deemed that I was incapable of making decisions regarding who to divulge this hideous secret to. Surely, if I were to recapitulate what had really happened to a visitors' list of well-wishers, it would only start manifesting the idea again in my mind and lead to a further attempt. Well, considering I couldn't even wipe my own arse for a solid month, I don't think sprinting to the nearest dual carriageway was much of a possibility. In my mind, I had made the most rational decision I could by trying to end what I deemed to be a fruitless existence. The striking heartache of an 18-year-old deciding they are not worthy of the oxygen they breathe any more still hits me even now. What probably resides with me even more so on a daily basis, is how on earth the devastating physical impact of being struck by a vehicle moving at that speed, in that environment didn't land me six feet under almost instantly?

I adapted very quickly to the uncomfortable surroundings I was in and by about week 4 of the holiday from hell (that has Channel 5 Sunday night documentary written all over it) I began to very gently and very gradually acknowledge the very obvious fact; I was still alive. It was a ceaseless and pointless task establishing exactly how and why I was still breathing. I had to now consolidate the jagged, misfit pieces of energy I did have into the best damn jigsaw puzzle I could muster. I remember the stern conversation I had with myself (I'm not the world's best conversationalist, but it was either talk to myself or instigate some juicy gossip with the catheter most days) about understanding my situation and the magnitude of it, which I was just slowly starting to appreciate.

"You've been given a chance here, Laura. A completely unbelievable, unimaginable chance. Fine, you'll have to live with the fact you are slightly more deformed and wonky than you were before, but Jesus Christ, don't waste this moment. Don't waste this freedom, for freedom is the choice to struggle with what you want, not what you have to. Shall we be blunt? You should be dead, Laura. That lukewarm chicken curry that has been sat next to your unused bedpan for 45 minutes might taste like cardboard marinated cotton wool but putting food into your mouth, chewing it and digesting it is a privilege you didn't even realise you had and could have completely lost. Do everything, see everything, *feel* everything, fail at everything, get up and try again at everything and achieve everything you can, day, after day, after day. All of the things you should have missed out on, all of the things that should never have been obtained (had the most probable outcome have actually occurred) you need to go and fucking do. You shouldn't bloody be here, Laura – if you live for another 6 months it is a gift." That age-old piece of advice, 'life is precious', means nothing at all until that cherished existence is threatened and endangered in such a way, you completely revalue it. I'd been obstinately trying to end something that hadn't really even begun and I barely even realised.

I may well have been a walking, talking body of scars and unorganised trauma, but that was my realisation; I was walking and talking; two of the most regular, ordinary human faculties I still possessed (only just) that we all undervalue every day. If they were all I was left with then I'd walk around the coastline of the country, every single country and talk incessantly about what I was doing in all of their respective languages. The initial months of my recovery never once allowed the possibility of imagining anything more than my walking adventure. The prospect of swimming, cycling, running, climbing, kayaking, kicking, weight-lifting, abseiling, front abseiling, boxing, throwing, punting, rowing, fell-running, orienteering, jumping, pushing, pulling and just about any other active, adrenaline-fuelled verb you could think of was so far out of the question it wasn't even worth asking. If I would have said, in between dressing changes and anaesthesia questionnaires, to the marvellous team of individual medical professionals caring for me throughout that recovery process,

"Just so you know, in 10 years' time I'm going to take this gammy leg of mine and all my other physical and psychological broken parts and put them back together with damn Gorilla Glue if I have to. Then I'm going to run 10 marathons in 10 consecutive days in 10 different locations in the UK and raise thousands of pounds for the life-saving charity that gave me a lift here the other day. Then I'm going to write a book about those 10 years, 10 marathons and everything else in between (preferably on a laptop because of my broken hand) and hopefully inspire other people not to land themselves in the monumental shit state I seem to currently be in."

They would have attempted their best pitiful smile, rushed some more sedative through my veins and sent yet another concerned email to the psych team regarding my 'Delusions of Grandeur.' Whatever my delusions appeared to be to them, they weren't delusional. They were opportunities I couldn't wait to embrace and grab by the balls. I'd passionately flirted with the fragility of life and categorically didn't want a second date. When you have come so close to death, every day is a bonus. Yesterday, today and tomorrow and every day are absolutely no different.

Chapter 1.

17:18

That time will forever be ingrained in my memory. 18 minutes past 5pm on Friday 12th November 2010. The repetitive blinking colon between the 4 numbers on the24-hour digital clock display of my beloved Ford KA was, strangely, the only calming focus I had, in my otherwise intensely stressful headspace. Despite the extraordinary psychological discomfort I was enduring in that moment, there was also a paradoxical sense of peace, knowing that I was finally about to take control of my dire situation. Despite the fact I could still use my sense of sight, it had appeared, for the use of my taste, touch, hearing and smell, that I had gone into a bizarre world of sensory deprivation. My focus in that moment was so ardently channelled into what I wanted to do, what I needed to do, I could have been standing out in the wintery conditions, completely naked and probably not felt a thing. The pitch-black eeriness of the A14 was only periodically being lit up by rush-hour headlights, so as long as I kept out of their glaring beam, the being completely naked option may well have gone unnoticed.

Friday, November 12th 2010 was a very typical late winter evening. It was cold and blustery outside. Little speckles of rain decorated my windscreen in a polka dot pattern, each one refreshing and reinvigorating the dirty, dusty edges of my neglected vehicle. I was startled at how strong the wind was. It was intermittently moving my defenceless little Ford KA with each and every gust. Whoosh. Whoosh. Whoosh. I thought my handbrake was going to give up and I was actually going to be blown back out into the road from the desolate lay-by I'd parked in, at junction 36 westbound of the A14 dual carriageway. It was a wonder I could actually notice weather conditions at all. My battered, bruised mind still entirely hypnotized with such a detailed plan to kill myself, it was allowing no room for anything else. I was numb. Void of feeling. Void of emotion. Void of most of my rational thinking. It wasn't until I tried to snap out of this brainwashed state and actually moved my fixed vision away from the digital display of my dashboard, that I realised the violent movement of my car wasn't wind at all. It was the busy stream of lorries, trucks and other vehicles that I had planned to walk into. It now made sense why I thought it had been so windy. The abrupt jolting I had been experiencing was each and every car, van or lorry that was skimming past me as I sat motionless in my car.

'Fuck me,' I thought.

'Those lorries are powerful enough to move a stationary car and I'm about to walk out in front of one. What the fuck is it going to do to me?'

Kill me, hopefully. Or that was the plan, anyway, a plan that had been manifesting itself long before that fateful evening. You see, to me, walking straight out in front of an articulated lorry, travelling at 60 mph on a dual carriageway wasn't irrational thinking at all. It was a master plan that had infiltrated every minute of every day for weeks and weeks. It had kidnapped my brain and wouldn't release it until it had been lived out in its full glory. It had, quite perversely, become my next challenge. It was my main focus. As if I was going to get a bloody medal, T-shirt and goody bag at the end of it. My main focus at 18 years and 4 days old had become to commit suicide by walking out in front of a lorry. It has always been that near-obsessive focus, dogged determination and unrivalled drive I possess that has created both marvellous opportunities in my life, but also, landed me in rather precarious situations. If I say I'm going to do something, I'm going to do it, be it to my detriment or my advantage.

My plan began to unravel that afternoon whilst at Sixth Form College. Yes, I hear you. Why an earth would you attend a day at school if you wanted to kill yourself? Because that was in my plan. I had dedicated myself to this 'life-ending event' and I wanted to execute every part of my plan in exact detail. I was sat in a Sports Science lecture at the end of the day, despondent and argumentative, which was entirely out of character for me. I was typically gregarious. I was reliably the life and soul of the party. I often used my terrible humour and extrovert personality to cover up the other, less well-known side of my personality that I had developed a successful ability to hide, very well. The side of my personality (that everyone has) that you don't want anyone to see. Obviously, my teacher at the time picked up on this sudden personality change and kept me behind after the lesson. As much as this was completely not part of my plan (I intended to sneak away quietly at the ringing of the bell) I quite enjoyed this exciting twist.

'Let's put a cat amongst the pigeons.' This is what the obnoxious, self-indulgent 18-year-old me thought. 'Let's tell them exactly what I am about to go and do, have a herculean scrap with teachers trying to restrain me and then play cat and mouse with the list of authorities that would inevitably be called. Let's have a good old-fashioned pursuit around the back roads of Suffolk and properly go out with a bang.'

'What's wrong with you, Birdy? You are really not yourself today.'

A Head of Year and Deputy Head then also joined the classroom – apparently, word had spread fast about my sudden personality shift and I'd never been so popular. In the most nonchalant fashion, I said,

'I'm going to kill myself, Miss.'

Completely astounded but now paying fierce attention, she replied,

'What did you just say?'

'I'm going to kill myself. I'm going to drive to a lay-by on the A14 and walk out in front of a lorry.'

I was brazen, cocky, blaze, three characteristics the visibly fidgety staff would have never associated with me on a 'normal' day. In stark contrast to the members of staff that surrounded me, I was a picture of calm and composure and spoke those words as if I was giving my address to somebody.

'You are terrifying me now, Laura.'

Note the sudden change from the use of my well-known colloquial nickname to the serious formal address of my actual birth name which was only ever used when I'd been misbehaving or in some sort of emergency. I never misbehaved, never. So, it would appear the use of my formal name in that example was a combination of the two qualifying criteria for its use. They actually believed what I was saying; they seemed to know in that moment I was capable. Such out of character behaviour was certainly stirring a reaction in them that I had also not seen before. They were visibly anxious, a trait you very rarely see in any high-ranking teacher. Looking back, it must have been horrendous for those helpless teachers. My desperate disposition was not their fault, but I was convinced, because I'd disclosed my very specific plan, that it would have had to become their responsibility. Apparently, it wouldn't. I was pumped. The unplanned change of events left me ready for the onslaught of every adult within reaching distance to clamber on top of me and not let me move from the freshly painted classroom we were in. I could feel my heart racing in anticipation of the fight. But that highly-strung anticipation soon dwindled.

'You're 18, Laura, it is past school hours. I have absolutely no power to keep you here. I'm ringing your Grandfather immediately but, legally, there is nothing I can do to keep you here.'

An emphatic but incredibly strange wave of disbelief, confusion and relief nearly overwhelmed me. The exciting twist to my plan had now omitted the massive scrap with my teachers, but still maintained the additional cat and mouse plot I hadn't initially accounted for. I knew my Grandad would call the Police; I knew my plan to kill myself now had an unplanned time element to it. Not wanting to hang around for them to change their mind, I swiftly got up.

'See you on Monday, Laura,' my Head of Year bleated hopefully.

'No, you won't,' I belligerently replied. Belligerent is described as being, 'of warlike character; aggressively hostile.' That was so apt. I was heading to war. My head was nothing short of a battlefield at that point and I knew it wouldn't be long before I was taking a life. Not just any life. My own.

I was so focused. I was being totally encapsulated by my own suicide it almost became exciting. That is how desperate and deranged genuine suicide is. You are truly buoyant that the idea and tendencies that have consumed you for so long are finally being realised. There was literally no turning back now. As much as the sequence of events I'd had etched into my brain for months were flowing well, I had an added pressure now that I hadn't accounted for. I had to go and get the job done because the consequence of hesitating was now damaging to the plan. There was now the very real potential of ending up either in the back of a Police car or, worse, sectioned in a mental institution. The thought of anyone trying to stop me now, be it by legal authority, through duty of care or just because of genuine concern, wasn't even worth acknowledging. So, much as contemplating anyone else trying to control me during this planned final event, that I had complete control over, made me shudder.

I was pretty oblivious to the world around me as I left the school gates, however, not enough to not notice the confused glares of my fellow peers, as we bottlenecked into the subway. I was suddenly distracted. I could have done it there and then. Our school gates lead straight out onto a suitably dangerous main road – hence the subway.

'No, Laura. It's a 30mph limit. That won't kill you. Not a high enough risk. Too many people. Too much drama. A very high chance of survival. Stick to the plan.'

I was hanging off every word of the quite unbelievable self-talk I had developed and refocused my attention. I had unconsciously begun to dismantle my mobile phone – this explained the glares. I knew my phone could be triangulated if my SIM card remained in it and the phone stayed with me. Essentially, if the Police thought I was a high enough risk, they had resources that could track my phone signal to give a rather accurate location of where I was. I knew this was an important part of the plan but I didn't even realise my hands had started to do it. The steps had been rehearsed in my brain that many times, my body clearly just knew what to do next. It knew it had suddenly been thrown onto centre stage and had to perform. I took my SIM card out of the back of my phone and squeezed it in half between my thumb and forefinger. I squeezed so hard the circulation became restricted at the tip of my two digits, causing them to go a ghostly white which almost camouflaged with the white exposed plastic of the card. A thin streak of white spread across the diameter of the rectangular piece of plastic, as it began to snap at its now weakened core. I put the two halves of the SIM into one bin and the remainder of my phone in a separate one. You don't need to be a psychiatrist to recognise there is a serious problem if an 18-year-old is knowingly throwing their phone into a bin. Most would probably put their suicide attempt on bloody Snapchat nowadays. I also didn't want the distraction of relentless phone calls from distressed friends and family pleading with me to consider what I was doing. I had, almost instantaneously, transformed from the happy, confident persona I was on a daily basis into the self-indulgent, egotistical stereotype one would associate with a suicidal teenager.

I began travelling toward the A14 in quite a frantic and reckless manner. I was then displaying all the classic attributes of an audacious teenager with a carefree attitude, struggling inexplicably with their mental health. In 'ordinary' circumstances, I would have never driven dangerously. But this circumstance was now far from ordinary. In fact, every intense mile I travelled was getting further and further away from any sort of normality.

I soon found myself tearing down the A14, still conscious the Police could be on my tail, yet carefully considering which lay-by was going to be my final parking place. It took an hour of reckless driving, an hour of repeating senselessly in my mind, 'Not this one, the next one. Not this one. The one after next,' before I finally put my indicator on and pulled into a lay-by just past junction 36 Westbound of the A14. It was the most lonely and uninhabited place I'd ever been in for so many reasons. Of course it would be; lay-bys are not well known for their friendly company, modern safety measures or warm welcomes. They are for truck drivers to empty their bladders and impatient business people to pull over and answer their phone when the Bluetooth is playing up. There was no sight of even an isolated bird or scared rabbit to keep me company, or even empathise with me in the state I was in. Discarded litter was being hurled around in the wind, only being allowed to lay motionless for just a second before another gust sent it flying off into the night. The only protection between my car and the flow of traffic was the patchy white paint, partially worn off from the tarmac, distinguishing the start and end of the lay-by. Thankfully my unwavering focus on the task at hand was being disrupted by one thing. There was at least one other focus that was disturbing some of the negativity coursing through my brain, something else to momentarily distract me and it was that I desperately needed a piss. My full bladder, relentlessly pleading with me to be relieved, was at least bringing back some sensory feeling in this remarkable condition I'd found myself in.

'Just piss yourself.'

This was my first genuine thought. You are literally about to haul yourself in front of a lorry - you may not even be in one piece by the time you finish. What difference is it going to make if you are wet and stink of piss? Even in the depths of psychological turmoil that I was in, I was still concerned at the indignity of wetting myself and the lack of control it portrayed. I suppose I took a depraved sense of pride in being able to control my bladder, as I struggled to control any other psychological or physical aspect of my pathetic little life at the time. In reality - as is very often the case with people who take their own lives - this was actually far from the truth for me. I, to any other rational thinker, was not pathetic at all.

I had, only a few months previously, got 8 A*s in my GCSE's, I was playing football at County level, I'd already represented my country playing football at 15 years old, I had friends, I had an incredible Grandfather whom I adored, I was studying for my A-Levels, looking to go to University, I was fit, young and healthy. I was, arguably, at a very exciting and prosperous time in my life. And this is the exact problem we have always had and still have now, with recognising poor mental health. If I had a quid for every outdated, incompetent, inadequate doctor or NHS 'professional' that presented me with the same conundrum,

'How an earth could you possibly be so despondent, whilst living such a fruitful existence? Come on, you are young, pretty and healthy. Why would you *choose* to feel like this?'

The only unintentionally helpful word amid that sort of reoccurring sentence was 'choose.' In my mind, if I was indeed *choosing* to feel like I was, then I can choose not to feel like it as well. Unbeknown to me and them at the time, if only that avenue of thinking, the correct avenue, that we all actually have complete control over how we think and feel, could have been explored in a bit more detail, the insulting advice given from these professionals could have improved immeasurably. It was probably around the 3rd time I heard this line from different professionals that I lost faith in the mental health services of the NHS. This to me would suggest that I am not the only young person to walk out of a doctor's appointment, fiercely discouraged by the lack of competence and conviction in such a vital aspect of medicine.

Please don't get me wrong; I love the NHS. As an organisation, they are a Trojan workhorse, surmounting every obstacle placed in their path. It is one of the proudest assets and achievements of this country. But they are still failing when it comes to highlighting, diagnosing and treating mental health. In the years preceding and proceeding November 12th 2010, I lost count of the number of times I had to fill in another survey asking if I'd got dressed in the last week, if I had an appetite, if I had 'negative thoughts' or was asked to somehow attempt to place on a scale of 1-10 how I felt that particular day. How can you possibly quantify the nonsensical, deranged, perplexed but occasionally happy mess that was my brain and my daily outlook? What is the difference between a day being a 6/10 or a 7/10 or a -4/10? Which, unfortunately, the majority of days were at that point in my life. It is a near unimaginable task for someone, professional or not, to think up a universal, easy-to-use applicable tool or system to measure a person's daily mental health. I'm just suggesting that a numerical scale is really not an easy option to work with – even words would be easier. How was your day today? Not that shit at all, actually, pretty shit, really shit, unimaginably shit, so shit I am thinking about dying, the shittest it has ever been and I'm planning on dying soon. At least that way we could all relate to it a little bit better to the human being in question rather than attempting to interpret their psychological disposition using a sliding numerical scale.

A tragic yet frequent trend amongst those who do not feel worthy enough to continue is that they once significantly contributed to the joy that is popular culture.

Robin Williams, Robert Enke, Keith Flint, Caroline Flack, Chester Bennington, Alexander McQueen. The individuals that once lit up sports fields, cinemas or music stages are the same ones we now remember with such sorrow. I can't help but imagine that those individuals were greeted with the same ludicrous advice I had, from their shrinks or private doctors.

"Come on, Robin, how can you be depressed? People adore you; you make people laugh."

"You've got everything, Alexander, why would you want to throw that all away?"

The instant go-to of any ingenuous well-wisher is to focus on the materialistic assets in one's life– as if they act as some sort of motivation to stay alive. We, I believe, can derive from this that suicide can act as an incredible leveller. One's money, size of house, income, popularity, societal standing, social media presence, future prospects, family commitment all pales into insignificance when you can't control your mind. For the mind is the epicentre of your own personal universe. Of course, we cannot ignore those individuals at the other end of the social hierarchy, the suicides that you don't hear about, the 'suicide statistic-makers.' The sort of suicides that, unbelievably but undeniably, society would class as more justifiable. It is far more understandable for the poverty-stricken, homeless drug addict from inner-city London to kill themselves than it is the high-flying rock star, with adoring fans, who used 20-dollar bills to swat flies. It doesn't make your heart sink very far if or when you hear of another unloved, nameless, unknown soul wandering on to the train tracks to be flattened by an oncoming freight train. A story like that would barely make a halfway column in a local newspaper. But glance in the national news that another helpless young pop star has taken their life, and it grabs your attention and you can't quite believe it. Your heart sinks a lot further for the multi-millionaire whose tragic suicide story is publicised globally than the lonely track-wanderer and that is why we get it so wrong. Suicide is very rarely pre-empted by debt or societal standing, it is a desperate measure taken by individuals who perceive they have no control over their life, their mind or their current predicament; irrelevant of their bank balance or popularity. Having no control of the mind is exactly how my situation could be described.

The furious battle with my bladder continued as I sat alone in my KA, still being noticeably nudged by every vehicle that trundled past. The busy rush-hour traffic provided a loud hum outside of my car but I was immersed in a strange silence. I had managed to successfully (and quite significantly) neglect my self-worth, esteem and dignity enough to reach this point but I still couldn't bring myself to knowingly urinate in my own clothes, or slightly more acceptable, piss in a bush at the side of the road. There was still a glimmer of self-worth left. I wouldn't have to deal with the uncomfortable sensation for much longer. Arguably, one would suggest an individual, at the stage I was then at, would be completely void of rational thinking, almost at the point of emotional paralysis. But that small act of decency, to not succumb to my thoughts of degrading myself even further, would be contrary to that suggestion. I also wasn't quite at the stage of emotional paralysis either. As hard as I tried not to be, I was actually overcome with terror, a deep-rooted fear I had never felt before. I was violently shaking and about to vomit at any moment. For all those that wanted to convince me that I had lost my sanity and any form of rational thinking at that point, I absolutely hadn't. There was still a small morsel left. No insane individual would have been as scared as I was in that moment. I could still feel. I was still experiencing a relatively normal human reaction to the plight I was in. My fear at taking my own life in such a graphic manner was the only strand of normality left. For one diminutive moment, I wished I hadn't got rid of my phone. I wished for that one flicker of a second that I could call my best friend. I wished that there was someone next to me, pleading with me to rethink and reeling off every single reason why everything would be ok. But I'd come too far to look back now. I'd come too far to not finish the plan. I batted away that thought very quickly and focussed on what I needed to do.

I took one last glance at the digital clock on my dashboard, turned my heavy head left to have one last long stare at the suicide letters littered all over my passenger seat. The fact that I had to pluralise the word 'letter' would suggest I had more people rooting for me than I realised. But in that exact moment, recognising my ample support network didn't even creep into my highly concentrated brain. I gradually eased myself out of the relative comfort of the driver's seat to a standing position, clinging to my car door. I was about 3 metres away from the continuous stream of traffic I was headed for. I wanted to make sure it was a lorry that struck me. I needed to make sure I could see 4 beams of light that were illuminating from both the bottom and the top of the vehicle approaching, to ensure it was the giant, oncoming cab of a lorry. I'd come too far now not to execute the rest of the plan exquisitely. I couldn't jump in front of a measly saloon or estate car; not even a 4x4 would suffice, I'd established that wouldn't be enough when leaving the school gates (which seemed like a lifetime ago). Still trembling, I walked close enough to the side of the carriageway that I was now in reaching distance of the traffic. The force of the passing vehicles was so, so powerful; I knew my action had to be quick and meaningful. The shell of my 1-tonne car had felt the full effects of the heavy stream of traffic, let alone my 65kg frame that could barely stand up against the force of it. A blur of blue lights and sirens lit up the opposite side of the carriageway, momentarily derailing my focus. That Police unit may have been completely unrelated to me. But paranoia continued to tease me and I was convinced they were coming for me. I was convinced they would section me within seconds and my freedom would be taken and more importantly, my plan would fail. That Police car was the last push I needed. I looked to the right to see an oncoming lorry, with a clear path in front of it, nothing but me and the huge, fast approaching lorry. With every ounce of energy I could summon, I quickly walked, eyes wide open, directly into its path.

I remember nothing from that moment onwards. It was only through news reports and later conversations I learned of the unimaginable circus that had erupted on the dual carriageway on that wintery Friday night. I surmise that I can't remember a period of about 2 hours, either because my brain is still, 10 years later, trying to protect me from the horrific image of my mangled, motionless body sprawled on the side of a road by repressing the trauma or, due to the severe head injury I sustained, I suffered such tremendous concussion, there was going to be no chance of me recalling the night's events in any capacity. The A14 must have looked like the set of a BBC 1 Casualty Christmas Special. Police, Highways Agency and Ambulance all had an unwanted invite to the party. The cherry on top of a very undercooked and poor-tasting cake was the arrival of the East Anglian Air Ambulance. My condition was life-threatening enough that the short journey to Addenbrooke's Hospital warranted a helicopter journey and the heroic care provided by the doctors and critical care paramedics on board. Every single emergency and non-emergency service played their role in the Christmas special unravelling on that Friday night. The Police and Highways services were mere extras in the background compared to the star of the show, the East Anglian Air Ambulance. I strongly believe I owe my life to EAAA. Without their leading role, by effortlessly saving life and limb on the roadside, I'm quite sure I would have croaked it there and then. Due to the severe blood loss from the open fracture I had sustained to my right femur, the situation was entirely time-critical. Every second was (as the name would suggest) critical and a roadside ambulance did not have the equipment, expertise or experience required to deal with a list of injuries such as mine. It was very much touch and go for the first few agonizing hours. I was literally hanging on by a thread, just like my nearly amputated right thigh.

The first clear memory I have is waking up surrounded by doctors and nurses, unable to move. I felt like an interesting bug in the nursery playground, being prodded and poked by snotty kids, enthralled at the opportunity to roast me in the sun with a magnifying glass. Confusion, pure rage and terror were soon met with the sensation that I still needed to bloody piss. How an earth can the human body endure the turmoil I've just subjected it to and not lose control of its bodily functions? That was incredible really, the more I think about it. I managed to maintain the function of my bladder whilst also fighting for my life. What was not so incredible was a very matter of fact nurse informing me my bladder was full (no shit, Sherlock) and that she planned on imminently inserting a catheter. Being the massive closet lesbian I was at 18 years old, I should have been jumping at the chance of a charming young nurse attempting to relieve me in an intimate area, but, funnily enough, I wasn't too enamoured by the idea. That very uncomfortable moment ensured, from that day forward, I never, ever again took for granted the sensation of needing to wee. Cathy the Catheter and I became very well acquainted and I wouldn't feel that welcome sensation of actually needing to piss for the following 5 weeks, not even once. Cathy did all the hard work in that department for the duration of my hospital stay.

Obviously, I couldn't personally see the desperate physical state I was in, however, my father's reaction when he walked up to the hospital trolley I was laid in told me all I needed to know. Before he could even speak, the colour seeped from his face and he had to immediately walk out again. Apparently, seeing a giant flap of your 18-year-old daughter's scalp hanging from her forehead is enough to send even the most committed father to regurgitate his lunchtime sandwich. My Harry Potteresque scar was beginning to create itself just nicely. I can remember being stubbornly defiant to every single suggestion that was being made to me.

"Calm down, Laura, you are going to be ok."

But that was the main problem everyone around me kept ignoring. At that moment in time, the one thing I didn't want was to be ok.

"JUST LET ME GO. LET ME FUCKING GO."

I was adamantly fighting against being saved. Even at that point. I didn't mean, 'let me go' as in allow me to discharge myself from the hospital (which would have made for interesting viewing given half of my right thigh was still laying on the A 14 somewhere). I meant 'let me go' as in let me die. Stop administering whatever life-saving treatment you are giving and allow me to be exactly what I wanted to be. Dead. I was like some sort of caged animal trying to pull out wires, trying to move, attempting to undo any maintenance work that had already been done. This was entirely futile in itself, because my destroyed little body, as hard as it tired, really couldn't achieve much at all. But I was still pouring every ounce of energy I had into achieving what I had set out to achieve. The gentle, patient doctors that were calmly trying to soothe the near-deranged state I had achieved, understandably resorted to plying me with ketamine to not only ease the pain, but just ease the suffering in general, for everyone involved, not just me.

I was still drifting in and out of consciousness as I was wheeled down to the first of my surgeries for that night – I ended up having 11 in total. This was just the first attempt to reconstruct my then completely deformed, de-skinned, destroyed right leg. Despite my infrequent lack of consciousness, I very quickly came to the realisation then, not only did I have to continue to face the life that I was so desperately trying to end, I also had to do it with life-changing injuries. My plan had catastrophically failed in my eyes, however very cautious doctors still informed my father and grandfather of the dangerous medical position I was in;

"The next 24 hours are crucial. We can't confirm whether she will make it through the night yet."

Of course, being the stubborn brute that I was (and still am), I made it through night 1 and night 2 and night

3. I have very little memory of days 1-5, which I suppose is probably a good thing. I had bizarre recollections, almost hallucinogenic images (I probably should have enjoyed that whilst it lasted) of unrecognisable individuals hovering over my bedside, empathetically trying to get a response or some sort of vocabulary out of me. You know when they pixelate the face of some thug on Crime Watch and you can't quite fathom who they are? That was all I could see for a solid 72 hours. I do remember receiving a thorough instruction to press the inviting green button placed in my hand every time the pain started to engulf my entire body again. It took maybe a couple of minutes for the thing to charge up and turn green again and it stayed green for about as long as the most irritating set of traffic lights you know. So, predictably, it stayed bright racing green for about a nanosecond before I had to hit it again. It was quite necessary for me to be up to my eyeballs in morphine for the next memorable procedure (that I can recall) to take place.

There is a curious little scar, made up of 4 small circles, that sits on the left side of my neck as you look at it, which has been terribly mistaken on many occasions for a love bite. A bloody love bite? How anyone would make that mistake is beyond me. But, if ever in any doubt of the nature of my scar, or whether anyone would have given me a love bite at the time, or at any point leading up to that time, please refer to the following.

A. I really don't think anyone would be that desperate

B. I literally must have looked like a hung-over corpse at that point.

C. My blood was so full of mess you really wouldn't want to be sucking that shit to the surface.

D. Please refer to A.

It most certainly isn't a love bite; it is a permanent physical reminder of the night I had to have intravenous antibiotics and pain relief inserted into my neck. Basically, the veins are larger in the neck and it would allow the distribution of whatever drug is going into your system to be a lot quicker than a normal intravenous line. But I wouldn't wholeheartedly recommend it. I was being pretty abrasive to anyone that came near me, irrelevant of their intentions. So, when the suggestion of 4 giant tubes being stuck into my neck started manifesting itself, I wasn't too pleased. I felt like a petrified lab rat being painfully prodded and poked whilst the experimental doctors laughed on in the background. This was, of course, not the case, but as the black and blue patterned skin of my face and head was being held still, the line sharply protruded my skin and the clinical taste of medicine burnt the back of my throat. Those 4 tubes stayed there for 4 days whilst they got me 'out of the woods' so to speak. However, I can at least now really empathise with anyone that has been bitten by a vampire. Thankfully, it wouldn't be long before I drifted off again, dreaming of the big green button, trying to make out which pixelated face was talking to me next.

As painful as the love bite tubes were and whatever was being pumped through them, they began to work and I started to regain full consciousness by around day 5 or 6. The childlike, frail and vulnerable streak of my personality that I never usually allowed to come out slowly came to the surface. I was still an 18-year-old kid, after all. I may have been legally an adult but, legal adult or not, at the first sign of something that resembled an appetite, all I wanted was a bowl of Coco Pops and someone to feed them to me. It took me around 40 minutes to get through the bowl which consisted of no more than about 5 spoonfuls of cereal, but it was something. It became very apparent that it was actually far more manageable to be in the semi-conscious state I was in a few days ago, clinging to the green button, totally unaware of what was going on around me. In reality, I'd had a blissful 5 days of intensive care. Anything would have been preferable to having to accept the predicament I was in. But still, bed-bound and in a pretty bad way, onwards and upwards was my only choice.

A very poignant memory from the very fractious few days in hospital was the first conversation I had with my brother, following what I had done. Matthew and I had formed a somewhat unbreakable bond stretching into the latter stages of our adolescence, a bond created through a combination of empathy and resilience that we had both developed from sharing a similar upbringing. We had each other throughout childhood and we, albeit subconsciously, leaned on and relied upon one another.

We both employed the same role in the sibling relationship; we acted as the dependable family member to each other as they were apparently so scarce elsewhere in the family tree. We had shared numerous football pitches and anxiety-ridden evenings together, we shared an appreciation for one another and fought and bickered just like any other siblings. Yet we never really talked in depth about what was going on, because we were sort of experiencing it concurrently. There was no need to discuss our worries and our concerns because we were living them together on a daily basis. His departure to University was long after our younger childhood memories together, but he made the very suitable decision to be as far away from the confusion and constant disappointment of home as he could and studied his degree in Hull. It was quite a distressing sound hearing him uncontrollably crying on the other end of the phone. I'd never heard him like that before. Of course, I tried to soften the mood asking if he was having onions for his dinner, but he abruptly cut me short, emphasising how serious this was and how utterly oblivious he was to the way I was feeling. I think 99% of the people around me would have suggested this was the very last thing they would expect 'someone like me' to do. I was a master of deception when it came to concealing my real feelings but my brother was clearly distraught that I'd reached this decision without so much as a nod to him to say I wasn't feeling well. I continued to mask how much I was truly suffering to him whilst he was on the phone. I didn't want to add to his already significant concern by revealing the daily pain and indignity I was enduring. He was just a year into a University degree which had all the stressors of a new home, a new way of life, a new degree, a new friendship group and the task of finding your way back to halls whilst blind drunk 5 times a week. He didn't need the addition of his very mentally unwell sister creeping up on him in a suicidal outburst. There was very little he could have done in the situation anyway but his avid helplessness was clear just from the tone of his voice. I assured him I was ok (even though I quite clearly wasn't) and that he shouldn't worry. But as soon as that phone call ended, I was digging myself further down into the emotional pothole that I couldn't get out of most days. I spent that night vividly imagining the phone call he might have had, along with many other family members and friends, should my attempt have been 'successful.' I shudder saying that phrase; it is the most incongruous, offensively blunt way of describing a person's death. Their suicide may have been successful in their own distorted mind, but to describe someone taking their own life as a successful attempt is surely the biggest oxymoron going. If success is measured by one's progression, development and one's ability to adapt and overcome life's hurdles, this was the most unsuccessful I'd ever been in my life. The despair I'd also caused my brother was an unwelcome addition to the categorical failure I felt at that time.

Chapter 2.

Rehab

For most, if you mention the word 'rehab', it instantaneously conjures up images of a skeletal Amy Winehouse, slowly draining the life out of herself, with a whole supportive nation gripped by her very visible despair, whilst all, at the same time, willing her to recover. It encourages notions of individuals who have become addicted to a substance that now governs their life and every decision within it. You think of drug addicts, alcoholics, gamblers, sexual predators, even those suffering with anorexia or bulimia to an extent. However, Addenbrooke's Hospital, which was then my home for 5 weeks, would begin to act as a rehabilitation hub in more ways than one. I may not have been addicted to drugs or alcohol, but even at that age, I was certainly controlled by consistent, self-destructive, unhealthy urges that I was trying to mask with excessive physical training, sport and an untamed extrovert personality. That extrovert personality, which had already taken quite a substantial knock, would, unfortunately, be no match for the barrage of criticism, analysis and judgement I was about to face. I didn't have control over my own bowels or bladder, let alone controlling any other aspect of my life. As always, however, no matter how dire the situation I found myself in, I knew they couldn't take my mind. They (or the situation) could strip me of my dignity, pride and resilience but nothing was taking control of my mind. That was and always will be mine; no one can take control of that. I just needed to realise it.

It infuriated me when I was told by more well-meaning mental health professionals, who pitifully sat by my hospital bed, that I had done what I had because I was depressed. Within minutes of meeting me and incorrectly 'analysing' me, that would always be their invalid conclusion. Yep. You take the easy route. You attribute my incredibly unique behaviour to the easiest label that matches up with your very generic textbooks. You tick your boxes and caress your little statistics (as well as your egos) and dispatch me as yet another entitled, attention-seeking teenager, with greasy hair, that doesn't give you eye contact, doesn't eat or sleep particularly well so, therefore, must be clinically depressed.

No. I fucking wasn't.

I wasn't just another woeful, pathetic, teenage suicide attempt that had swallowed 3 paracetamol and called an ambulance for a cuddle, a cup of tea and a night in A and E. And for the record - my hair was greasy because the destroyed nerve endings in my right arm weren't allowing me to lift my arms above eye level for more than about 3 seconds. If I wasn't going to allow myself to piss in my own clothes at the very brink of suicide, self-care and self-hygiene were clearly relatively high on the priorities list. That was, of course, one of the easiest criteria for them to tick off. Greasy hair? Worn the same trackies for 3 days? Tick and tick - you must be depressed. My hair was greasy and I had worn trackies for at least 5 days before they were washed for 18 years. But that was because I was too engrossed in chasing a football around for 23 hours a day, not because I was neglecting my personal hygiene or self-care and, therefore, must have been depressed. I was every level of mental unrest imaginable but 'depressed' was the easiest most convenient label for them to stick on me before hurriedly going to categorise the next individual; categorise the next individual but not actually provide any reassurance or advice to partner their hurried diagnoses.

I handed my A-Level coursework in 3 days before I attempted suicide. I went to football training 2 nights before I attempted suicide. I celebrated my 18th Birthday 4 days before I attempted suicide and had a great night as the life and soul of the party - from what I can remember. I was not depressed. I was craving power and control that I deemed I had very little of. I may have felt worthless, but I got up and gave life the best bloody good kick in the balls I could every single day. I never, ever lay in bed all day, neglecting the daily human decencies of hygiene or fresh air. I thrived off physical activity. I successfully and gracefully interacted with all forms of humanity on a daily basis. I held down a customer-facing part-time job whilst studying for 4 A-levels. I did have future dreams and ambitions, I just wasn't sure I was capable, worthy or noble enough to obtain them. I literally had no similarities with the general definition of depressed, nor did I display depressed behaviour, apart from maybe the 1% of the day when I hid from the world. That 1% of my life was not a justified percentage to work their conclusions from. And it was not worthy of the labels they were throwing my way. If I, as an 18-year-old adolescent, could spot glaring errors in their work and numerous flawed aspects of their assessments – why could no-one else?

It is so much easier for so-called 'professionals' to label a human being as something they have plucked from their Diagnostic and Statistical Manual of Mental Disorders, than actually do some fucking work and pick apart their mental thought processes and the fixable flaws within it. Yes, I was a rather volatile 18-year-old who had just thrown herself under a lorry. And yes, there is not a mental health department in this country that isn't drastically understaffed and overworked with barely even 5 minutes to fart. But I was also intelligent, educated and had a very solid holistic understanding of myself and what I wanted. Through the haze of frustration and resentment, I didn't acknowledge at the time that the incomprehensibly naive team of mental health workers were inadvertently, very slowly facilitating my recovery. I was beginning to feel something again. I was angry. I wasn't numb anymore; I was passionate about something. I wanted to fight against an incorrect, under-researched label they were trying to apply to me and my mental state. I wanted to fight for a decent, research-based, applicable mental health diagnosis that provided solutions, not endless problems. Even though I was outnumbered, insulted and humiliated, I, albeit subconsciously, began to fight for myself. I was worth more than their incorrect, belittling assessment. The battle with NHS mental health services had begun.

I was interrupted on a daily basis by similar professionals, spurting their nonsense about reading a book to distract you from your thoughts or flicking an elastic band whenever negative thoughts would intrude, or writing down your feelings; all, may I add, totally vague, useless, unsupported and undirected pieces of advice. I would entertain their babble with acknowledging smiles only for so long, just to get rid of them, normally. Not once did any one of them actually ask what I aspired to be, what I was good at, what made me feel powerful, one positive aspect of my day, one positive aspect of my life. Not once did they ever introduce the idea of gradually building a future, even if it meant spending my time gently researching jobs or Unis. Their prior concern was fuelling me with inaccurate, dated advice on a condition I strongly believed I didn't have.

One of the most unbelievable parts of it was, because I had so many different workers visit me in hospital, I was made to explain to each and every one what I had done and why I had done it. What an utterly incompetent and provoking question to ask. Clearly, I hadn't popped to the A14 for a sponsored litter-pick, had I? And why were they not communicating with one another? Why should I keep doing their work for them? It would have been so refreshing, so reassuring, so settling if, on just one occasion, a brash and overconfident individual walked in the room and said,

"Well, clearly you didn't think you'd be having this conversation today because you've gone out of your way to try and kill yourself, but you failed miserably so shall we crack on and start doing the best with what we've got? Tell me one good thing that has happened so far today and we will build from there!"

I would have undoubtedly interacted with a person if they had a cracker of an entrance like that. I needed someone real, someone gutsy and bold enough to actually criticise my negative and incorrect thought processes and decisions, yet be supportive and professional enough to work through a way of improving them.

But no, instead you get rather pathetic, softly spoken, feeble individuals that look like they could do with a good bloody meal and makeover themselves, who all have an unrivalled desire to live in the past and drag you back through it, as well as muttering their nonsense so quietly and incoherently they may as well be talking Swahili. Obviously the softly, softly, gently, gently approach is a ploy to not upset you or offend you in anyway, because their main focus is covering their own arse and following an outdated textbook and guidelines as opposed to actually helping. Softly, softly, gently, gently has never really helped anyone. Someone suffering as outwardly as I was should have been told what they needed to hear, not what they wanted to hear, and that takes courage. Someone with the bravery to risk offending someone and also risk a bit of confrontation can achieve so much more in the long run. It appeared, in my experiences, that many, many so called mental health professionals were so lacking in that crucial personality attribute.

One very obvious positive that was never properly appreciated or recognised by the plethora of professionals I came across was how hard I worked whilst I was hospitalised. My drive, ambition and focus had been so strong before it was cathartically (but rather tragically) released within a suicide attempt and it appeared the lorry wasn't forceful enough to knock those qualities out of me completely. I craved something positive to cling on to, and it was obvious to me that the self-healing process and searching for my own mental wellness was becoming my only option. I kept being advised by my mental health 'professionals' that working academically in hospital might add unnecessary stress to my already rather agitated situation. But this was yet another poorly thought-out, generalised, unjustified piece of advice that I conjured up plenty of reasoning to ignore. I needed some dignity and structure to my day. I needed some tiny level of achievement out of the 24-hour-a-day shit storm I was weathering daily. Even if I managed 20 minutes of revision a day between anti-blood clot injections and bed baths, I'd achieved something; something worthwhile and something to give me a small boost of pride which had been non-existent for weeks. The professionals surrounding me quite clearly couldn't see the fantastic logic I was using just 10 days after throwing myself in front of a lorry and maintained their strong desire to constantly focus on what had been, not what was about to come. They continued with their ill-educated advice to not worry about school work, again ignoring the fact that school and exams were never, ever a contributory factor to my poor mental health; education was actually one of the biggest positives in my life. They continued to ignore the person sat in front of them whilst I was frantically emailing teachers left, right and centre to build my self-worth with good honest hard work and education. I undertook my own version of self-care and adopted a forward-thinking approach to recovery, whilst the trained individuals around me insisted on talking about what had been and gone. We can write War and Peace about my dance along the A14, love, but that's not going to pass my A-Levels and start carving a path to a better future, is it? You fucking moron. How about I deal with the factors that led me to this bed-ridden mess, whilst also constructing a vision for the future, however long that may last, and actually give some purpose to my existence as opposed to being the waste of oxygen I feel I am currently? My A-Level examinations were 6 months after I tried to take my own life and I achieved an A* and 2 A grades in the subjects of English Literature, Sports Science and Psychology. I am convinced to this day that my commitment to work during and after my hospital vacation was a huge foundation for my final grades. It would appear my approach to recovery after a suicide attempt trumped the professional approach yet again. Had I taken their advice, I guarantee you I'd be climbing the walls in a funny farm, having been in there for 10 years, still being spoon-fed daily their ridiculous guidance and recommendations, still wondering why I hadn't passed my A-Levels at the age of 27.

I recall a very prominent memory of a home-based rehabilitation session with a mental health professional, who had all the features of a poor man's Whoopi Goldberg. The point of her visit was to try and encourage slightly better sleep. The PTSD (Post Traumatic Stress Disorder) was already violently embedding itself into my nightly routine just weeks after the night of the incident. I'd never experienced anything so disconcerting in my sleep ever before. At least 5 to 6 nights a week, I was experiencing vivid, destructive nightmares, envisaging the events of that night and replaying them in an awful production in my sleep. I experienced a recurring nightmare where either someone I cared about, or I myself, would be hit by a lorry, waking up at the point just after they had been hit. Often, they were so vivid, I'd awake so distressed, unsure for a few seconds whether what had just occurred in my dream was actually reality."Whoopi" was hopefully visiting to provide advice around this problem as I avidly refused to ever take any form of medication. If I want to improve an aspect of my psychological well-being, I want to be the one responsible for doing it. I want to work at it to improve it. Medication for managing mental health is another unbelievable copout. The minute you start relying on anti-depressants to improve your mood, you immediately invalidate yourself. You instantaneously agree that you have no power within yourself to improve your situation or mindset. Therefore, once you inevitably start to feel better after popping pills for a few months, you attribute your better mood to the medication you've been swallowing every day. It couldn't possibly be that you are starting to put more effort into being more positive or have started doing more exercise, for example. You dedicate your happiness to the little box of pills, depower yourself and your ability and then your happiness becomes dependent on those pills. Then you're hooked. Not for me.

Whoopi began in her condescending tone,

'How are you today?'

She was clearly asking about my welfare through obligation, not genuine concern.

Woah, hang on now, Laura. That is quite a sweeping judgement to make of Whoopi; you have barely even met her!

I'll explain why I came to the conclusion that Whoopi didn't really give a shit and was, yet again, just going through the motions of her written-down responsibilities. If Whoopi did have some vague interest in her next home call, you would assume that at the very least she would have read my notes – the ones that she would have 100% had access to. She would know that just a couple of months previously, the young woman sat in front of her had attempted suicide by walking into the path of an oncoming lorry on a busy dual carriageway. You'll understand my judgemental nature when, during her sleep lecture, she came up with the bright idea of 'going for a walk' when I felt low. Please consider that I lived 5 minutes away from the A14 at the time. Also, please bear in mind I'm still being held up by crutches at this point and furthermore, I was still hugely psychologically vulnerable.

"Sorry, can you repeat what you just said?" I asked, astounded.

"Exercise is really good for clearing your mind and will help to fatigue you slightly to prepare for better sleep." She read perfectly from her mentally ingrained textbook.

"So, just to clarify, when I'm low (potentially suicidal), your professional advice is that I should go out on a walk?"

"You don't have to go far and there are other options if that isn't something you like the sound of or can physically do right now."

I was absolutely gobsmacked. I didn't want to be rude but I rather abruptly asked the question,

"Have you even read my notes? Do you have any idea of the reason I'm struggling with sleep?"

Clearly, it wasn't a very common occurrence for vulnerable, timid, brain-washed mental health patients to question and dispute the professional sat in front of them. I didn't need her to answer that question; it was strikingly clear what the answer was. Maybe my expectations were too high. The NHS were, and still are, under a lot of pressure and understanding and treating mental health is a whimsical minefield of uncertainty (it actually doesn't have to be but we'll address that later). I often question whether, had I taken her advice that night or any other night and been drawn to the tempting lull of the traffic on the A14 again, would anything have happened? Would her visit or her advice have been thoroughly scrutinised and pulled apart by a board of professionals? Would anyone have taken responsibility? Or would it have just been another preventable suicide, totting up the statistics, not given the time of day it deserves? Thankfully for me and for Whoopi, I don't know. I'll never know and neither will she. All I do know is I now can't watch Sister Act without becoming inexplicably enraged every time.

If I was to attempt to adopt a real rehab persona, to really embrace the experience, I'd suggest in comparison, a physio coming round to visit was like getting a shot of methadone. I couldn't wait for it. A professional person I respected and was overjoyed to see considering I had been bedridden for 3 weeks now. So, in a peculiar way, the experience I was having did replicate rehab. I had been physically deprived of my drug (exercise and sport) and emotionally deprived of the addictive, destructive behaviours that had landed me in this very predicament. So, therefore, a visit from the physiotherapist was a gateway to getting back some form of my drug. It was very exciting; I wondered what broken body part the lovely physio was going to come and fix on that particular day. Maybe they were coming to rub my cracked rib? Give me exercises for my broken femur? Strengthen my broken hand? Give me management exercises for the excruciating pain that was a partial skin graft on my right thigh? Whatever the plan was, it would break the monotony of repeats of 'Homes under the Hammer' on the 12-inch hospital TV that I could pretty much lip sync by now. However, I did hope every session would be finished by 12:30, for my lunchtime 'Loose Women' fix. I quite enjoyed the hour of nonsensical female conversation over my stewed goat and mashed turnip for lunch. I'm sure the NHS didn't serve up goat for lunch – I still hadn't really much of an appetite then so it is anyone's guess what the meat was.

It is a very normal occurrence for me to think back to those physio sessions at the start line of every physical challenge I undertake to this day. Every single time I have limbered up for a swim, a bike, a run or just to get out for a walk, I think of that very first physio visit. And I will tell you why. They literally sat me up and stood me up, like a manikin on the production line. Slowly and unsteadily, I agonisingly crutched myself, 1-legged, the 3 metres to the door of the segregated room I was in. For an extra treat, I had also been segregated in a room, completely on my own from the second week of being in hospital because I picked up a cracking case of 'Clostridium-difficile.' Basically, I was being uncontrollably sick and shitting myself because of a bacterial infection and I couldn't risk passing it on to any other patients. Thankfully, social isolation was just the pick me up I needed in week 2. The combination of contracting this delightful strain of bacteria as well as being near enough bed-bound up until that point also meant having to have your own backside wiped 3 or maybe 4 times a day. That was an unforgettable low point. Just when I thought I'd be getting through my day quite nicely, the uncontrollable urge to shit took over again. Consciously having another human being perform such an intimate act when you are already severely lacking in any pride or dignity was enough to bring me to tears on most occasions. It didn't matter how many times I heard,

"Don't worry. It's our job; we've seen it all before."

It just threw me straight back to the floor of childhood. Being scared, intimidated, not even being in enough control to wipe your own arse. Not being cared for enough to achieve simple personal hygiene. Not being instilled with enough pride to make oneself presentable – even in a hospital bed. Frequently, holding back salty tears, terrified in the knowledge someone else has entire control over every feeling, emotion and decision you make. It is a lonely and desperate place to have no control over some of the simplest reliefs in life. Having a shit, in private, on a toilet and wiping your own arse is a privilege and to this day, I never take it for granted. You don't appreciate how utterly abundant life actually is with those small privileges until you have them taken away from you. Try 24 hours without running water and toilet paper and see how you get on. Then try 24 without electricity, a bed or clothes and buck your ideas up when you think you've had a bad day. Still had enough toilet paper and dignity to clean your own arse today? You are not doing too badly then.

The 3 metres to the door and back of physio session 1 were enough to absolutely ground me. I was literally blowing out of my freshly wiped arse after covering 6 metres. I couldn't get my breath and was visibly warm and panting. Just 2 weeks previously, I was an energetic, bouncy 18-year-old running around a football pitch and smashing out 5k runs for fun and all of a sudden, there was this pathetic little state. A full workout used to be a half an hour run and chucking some dumbbells around with my eyes closed but in the state I was in back then, 6 metres to the door was all I could manage. But, none the less, it was progress; I was out of bed and moving for the first time in 2 weeks. Although completely knackered, I gained more hope that I might actually walk again in those 20 minutes than I had done in 2 weeks. A small but quite momentous victory when you consider my biggest achievement for the last 2 weeks had been having just enough strength to roll down my compression sock and check the insatiable growth of my leg hair.

Funnily enough, they don't provide suicidal 18-year-old patients with razor blades. Can't imagine why! But even that blanket decision in itself, to not allow simple hygiene equipment because of the apparent risk to life, completely diminishes such a large aspect of one's psychological recovery. I was deemed too irresponsible to be in charge of anything sharper than a spoon. It was irrelevant the person you were for the 18 years before you succumbed to suicidal tendencies, you were still deprived of adult, dignified, self-worth-inducing decisions like when to shave your legs. You were to be judged and categorised as not safe, because one individual decision overrides any previous positive personality trait or any previous confident pattern of behaviour. Granted, a high percentage of mentally unstable patients would probably jump at the opportunity of slicing and dicing their forearms for mild entertainment. I reiterate I wasn't mentally unstable. I was desperate, daringly trying to ascertain some control over my life, seeking some sort of permanent solution to the unforgiving complication my life had become. Nevertheless, had I been given the responsibility of shaving my own leg (I didn't need to worry how hairy the other one was, it was covered in bandage) I'd have been thankful and accepted my responsibility dutifully and carefully. Anyway, slicing my forearms in my hospital bed would have been an even more woefully unsuccessful attempt at suicide than my first one; I didn't need to contribute any further embarrassment to the situation.

The morning of 1st December rolled around and this was the scheduled date to have the vacuum-assisted dressing that had been passionately caressing my leg for the past few days removed in surgery, and get the final patching up done. The vacuum pack machine was quite incredible really. It was as though my leg was a pile of holiday clothes that needed dramatically squashing before being rammed into the suitcase. However, it wasn't clothes that needed squashing into my case; it was a skin graft that needed moulding to my thigh to make up for what had been lost on the A14. I had gotten quite used to the brief journey along the clinical hospital corridors on my way to the operating theatre. I had 6 surgeries altogether in my 5-week hospital vacation, and there were still plenty to come. On that occasion, being wheeled along the wards, I felt a modest sense of relief that maybe I could start attempting to glue together the broken pieces when I was home. The dismantled vase that represented my existence at that moment could be glued back together again, it could proudly sit on a mantelpiece once again and one day it might even have some lovely roses sat in it. The surgery was successful for a fifth time and Vera the vacuum pack dressing had done her job. The body has an astonishing, innate inclination to repair itself as efficiently as possible and I was privileged to be able to experience this first hand. That sounds like the biggest oxymoron going, doesn't it? It's not that I was 'happy to be hurt', more that I was in a privileged position to have suffered life-changing injuries and experience the instinctive power of the body, as it begins to fight back whatever stress it has been exposed to and repair itself. I had seen and felt the fortitude and resilience of the human body. I'd experienced its unconscious ability to just 'get on with it' when the environment it's consumed in becomes increasingly painful or difficult.

Learning how to actually walk again was one of the most unusual experiences of my life. I had lost between 12-15% of the muscle tissue on my right leg, which only contributed to the peculiarity. I'd debated popping down to the A14 again to see if I could mop it up off the side of the road and stick it back on, but unsurprisingly I hadn't been successful. I had an 'intramedullary' metal rod inserted within the hollow of my femur bone and metal screws fixed behind my patella to reconstruct my shattered thigh bone. So, not only did placing one foot in front of the other cause considerable pain, but I was also completely unbalanced and totally uncertain on 2 feet. Colin and Claire, the crutches, were by my side for weeks and weeks. The real physical challenge started when I eventually returned home after my 5-week stay at Addenbrooke's (undoubtedly a 5-star experience on Trip Advisor by the way). Being in a house had all the comforts of home but no guiding gentle hand of a physio, no regular and monitored pain relief, no thorough protection from infection and a lack of tea and biscuits on tap. It meant I had to work things out for myself.

Being at home also meant actually seeing my deformed leg for the first time. Throughout my hospital stay, the dressings had only ever been changed in surgery. For five weeks, my leg represented a giant tampon, just with no stringy bit at the end. The day before my 'release', I had watched a skilful nurse intricately pull stitches out of the deep wounds on my right arm before patching them up again. If I thought the jagged scars on my arm were impressive, I'd seen absolutely nothing yet. Thankfully, my very good friend Alice had the most wonderful Mum who also happened to be a district nurse. I near enough lived at Alice's for the first few days after coming out of hospital which meant her Mum, Lesley, could have a good crack at the dressings on my leg. It also meant I could partially experience what it was to have a gentle, tender and dependable parental figure caring for me – which was more needed at that time in my life than I think I'd ever realised. Alice and her brilliant Mum made the transition from hospital to home as safe, sensitive and dignified as they could, and I can never truly repay them for what they both did for me throughout my recovery. They saved me in more ways than one.

A couple of days after being discharged, I was at Alice's and very tentatively had a shower (slipping over and breaking the other leg would have been jolly inconvenient at that time) and washed myself for the first time in 5 weeks, before Lesley could start trimming away the layers and layers of dressing. Like a disgusting game of pass the parcel, the bright white of every layer that came off became more and more stained with a mustard tinge of yellow with the occasional blob of claret. My body was excreting a rainbow of colours whilst trying to repair itself. The final layer of sticky gauze and bandage was gently peeled back and I instantly saw the excavated, jagged oval hollowed out of the side of my right thigh. It was distinctly overwhelming. My gaze would have been fixed on that aspect of my leg if it wasn't then distracted by the red raw skin graft donor site on the top of my thigh that looked and felt like the most severe case of sunburn I'd ever seen. To finish the 'trio of torment', I then viewed the further excavation sites at the top of my buttock and behind my knee, as well as the long, linear scar slicing vertically through my knee cap where the metalwork had been inserted. Lesley's compassionate eyes momentarily caught my fixed gaze as she asked,

'Are you ok?'

'Yeah, I'm fine,' I replied very quickly, lying through my teeth. I started to hyperventilate at not only the shocking state of my right leg and the agony it was causing me, but also the stark realisation that I was responsible for it. This daily, persistent conveyor belt of excruciating pain and discomfort was entirely self-inflicted. Nobody pushed me in front of that lorry; this was my responsibility and I had to deal with it.

In my opinion, this is the most significant issue we have with suicide and all the pitiful associations that come with it. There were numerous contributing factors to my decision to try and take my life. I was struggling to deal with and process my tormenting childhood, I was as gay as they come and had no idea how to start telling people, I was ashamed of who I was, I'd lost a friend and was riddled with guilt that it should have been me, I was convinced I had no future and certain I didn't want one. The vast majority of those factors were not my fault, but all of them were my responsibility. Terrible things happen in life. Sometimes, terrible things happen, repetitively, to the same person and they are rarely ever that person's fault, but as soon as they happen, they *become* that person's responsibility. It is not good enough to pity a person who has tried to commit suicide, kindly and gently persuading them that none of it is their fault. It is really unfortunate that a string of disastrous events may have occurred; that part isn't their fault. It is really heart-breaking that a person decided to take drastic measures to deal with the mess they found themselves in. And any decent friend would be more than entitled to be worried about their mate. But attempting to commit suicide was *their* personal responsibility. They made that decision and there would have been very little anyone could have done to prevent it from happening. Suicide is a choice. Arguably, it is a very desperate and despairing choice, but it is a choice, none the less. If someone else had been injured from me walking out into the path of a lorry, it would have been my responsibility. If the driver of the lorry had been traumatised by what I did, it would have been my responsibility. Had I been successful in my mission to end my life, the ordeal suffered by my friends and family would have been my responsibility. This is why we *need* to talk about suicide and we need to, occasionally, stick a rocket up the arse of the people who have attempted it. We need to stop wrapping them in cotton wool, teach them how to take responsibility for their actions and start focussing on rebuilding a future instead of pointlessly wallowing in their awful past. I'm probably coming across as a heartless bitch here, but I'm not. I'm combining empathy with practicality. Wallowing in self-pity, having friends cook you dinner and dropping a worried text in every 2 days will only last for so long, before you actually need to pick yourself up and start making, building and waving your own magic wand because no-one else will do it for you.

Going out on a limb here and at the risk of causing offence to those who have not taken responsibility yet (I intend to cause no offence), I can't understand the people, of whom there are thousands, who claim to have attempted to commit suicide 40-50 times. Being blunt (and I understand I don't have a leg to stand on here, quite literally) you're not doing it right if it has reached that number. The practicality around suicide is relatively simple. It really doesn't take much imagination to work out a way to end your life. Life is so precious, yet it is actually alarmingly easy to finish it. So, if you are on attempt number 43, you must know what you are doing is not going to be 'successful' and you are just craving some help or dare I say it, a kind word and a bit of attention. Again, going out on a limb, if an individual were that desperate, they would have been long gone before you even sent the concerned text as to why they hadn't shown up for work. If you have been suffering with depression, alcoholism, suicidal thoughts, anxiety, or any form of mental illness that is impacting on your ability to function for 10 years and it hasn't improved – you are not working hard enough. In my opinion, we need to be more ruthless when it comes to mental health. Sometimes, you need to give your mate a long hard cuddle and just listen. But more often than not, you need to walk in and boldly interrupt their pity party, turn the music off, shove them out of the door (without a party bag) and get them to start working a bit harder on recovery.

Accepting responsibility was a huge part of my rehabilitation and recovery. It takes courage, time and, above all else, a desire to improve and get better for yourself, nobody else. Because ultimately, who are you doing it for? Even now I'll have 1 day out of 7 where I put my 'feel sorry for myself' pants on and sulk for 24 hours. But I've created that environment for myself, so it is my obligation to get out of it, wake up the next day and put my positive pants on to have another crack at it. I held a monumental pity party for a good 3-4 years after having my fight with the lorry. Within those 4 years after my initial hospital admission, I returned to Addenbrooke's to have the gaping scar on my right leg reduced with the help of some plastic surgery. It felt as though I had metaphorically relapsed by returning to the place that deprived me of my addictions just a few years before. But as an already insecure young woman, I couldn't have my leg looking the way it did and pull off a pair of shorts. Christ, it looked like a half-eaten chicken drumstick in a pair of full-length leggings. On my return to the Cambridgeshire hospital in 2013, the plan was to reduce the scar on my leg with the most fascinating medical process I'd ever experienced. A very empty bag of saline was inserted into the original scar site (during operation number 9 of 11) and over a period of 2 months, more weekly saline was inserted into my leg to make the bag expand. Gradually (as is experienced in pregnancy or rapid weight gain) the skin on my thigh began to stretch, causing an excess of skin for the very clever surgeons to play with. That excess skin was then moulded over the glaring concave in my thigh (operation number 10) to leave a rather neater, more presentable linear scar. Again, I had to take full responsibility for the painful weeks of recovery that process required, as I myself had not only chosen to cover up a very noticeable physical reminder of my past – I was the one that put it there in the first place.

Chapter 3.
The 2 Big 'G's

It was my turn. I knew this day would be coming. My heart had been nearly pumping through my sky-blue primary school polo shirt all morning. There was no discussion to be had on the matter, every child had their turn and every child had their day. The eternally grumpy and stumpy dinner lady, clad in her pink chequerboard pinny, waddled over to the outdoor whiteboard, marker pen in hand. The whiteboard was drilled to a brick wall in front of our concrete football pitch. This meant it sat directly behind me as I stood proudly in goal, throwing myself on the floor after the tattered year 3 football like a possessed cat. I was grateful for the whiteboard being behind me; out of sight, out of mind. I could remain focused on using any conceivable body part possible to stop the ball from going in my net. But no matter how hard I tried, I couldn't stop dinner lady Doris from writing the name of the next teachers' class due for their lunch on the whiteboard, in bold blue ink. My focus on the all-important lunchtime kick around was decreasing as I knew Doris was edging imminently closer to the board. The high-pitched squeak from the felt tip of the pen gliding along the surface of the porcelain whiteboard sent a shiver through my nervous little body. I was so accustomed to sticking to the rules, being the perfect child, doing anything I could to impress authority, that the rebellious task I was faced with genuinely filled me with dread. There it was, the next class to be called in for their fish fingers, Smash mash potato and beans was....

"MR GUITE – YEAR 3"

The heavy burden that lay on my shoulders was to fearlessly approach the whiteboard and precisely rub out the 'U' and the 'E' of my favourite teacher's name to reveal' MR GIT'. This daily task was enough to cause complete uproar amongst a playground full of excitable children. It would become uncontrollable enough when there were high winds or there was a lost dog sniffing round the wooden play apparatus, never mind there being a swear word sprawled all over a completely visible surface for all and sundry to wet themselves at. The small act of rubbing out letters created the upmost hilarity for every single child that was lucky enough to see it. So, this was a big responsibility and I couldn't let them all down. Doris had barely put the lid on her pen as I stealthily strode over to the board, still mildly disgruntled by the fact I might concede a goal in the few seconds it would take me to complete my mission. Whilst the team of dinner ladies were distracted with the influx of children now sprinting through the single door entrance to ensure they get the crunchiest fish fingers, I took my chance. With a quick flick and a rub, the letters were gone and, as the raucous laughter erupted in the playground, I felt heroic. The famously brown nose that even in year 3 I was well known for had been wiped clean for 5 minutes and I almost enjoyed my rebellious streak. I revelled in briefly being queen of the castle, despite the fact my crown was earned through unspeakable insubordination. Needless to say, once the laughter had died down, I felt awful and as though I needed to ferociously apologise to the whiteboard, Doris and Mr Git. But it looked like I had gotten away with it, the perfect crime. My duty was done for at least another 2 months.

Mr Guite was a fantastic man. There could have been an abundance of reasons why he would be my favourite primary school teacher but unsurprisingly, the main one was that he set up the first-ever Gorseland Primary School Cross Country Running Club. His perfectly trimmed chestnut moustache and array of superbly coloured striped shirts were justification enough to be top teacher but to start a running club too? That's almost worthy of legend status. Friday lunchtimes would never be the same again. Despite the fact that most 5-11-year-olds dart around with copious amounts of energy from dawn until dusk, attempting to recruit the same demographic to run continuously for half an hour during their lunch break proved remarkably difficult. Being an active and PE-loving student of Mr Guite's year 3 class, I had no choice in the matter; I would be partaking in Cross Country Club whether I liked it or not. Inwardly, I was totally enamoured by the idea of being a member of my first running club at the age of 8. But, of course, to all my onlooking peers, I shrugged it off as a bothersome inconvenience. It was a vain attempt not to ruin my mediocre popularity any further by displaying my true enthusiasm for the overwhelmingly boring pursuit that is long-distance running. The trouble, I believe, with getting young people into all forms of running (not just the long-distance slog) comes from 2 main sources.

I am one of the biggest advocates for PE in every form being routinely embedded in the school curriculum for all ages. The importance of children empowering themselves through improving physical skills, motor skills and endurance should never be underestimated. Being able to tangibly measure a personal skill improving over time because of continuous and persistent effort is crucial for confidence, self-esteem and independence. Throughout childhood and into adolescence, in physical education we are taught how to kick a ball properly, hit a ball accurately, throw javelins, shot-putts, and discus and bring inanimate objects to life through the medium of modern dance. But we are not taught how to bloody run. The purest of all sports - that is a sport, don't forget, not just a mode of transport or a torture technique for the overweight kids at school - the main foundation of so many sports is running, yet we totally neglect the important task of teaching young people the technique and intricate details of how to do it properly. Why are we teaching the next generation how to serve in table tennis but not teaching them the dynamics of running, how to pace yourself or how to improve how efficient you are across a certain distance?

Granted, continuously pacing out laps around a school field certainly doesn't have the same attraction as smashing the shit out of a rounder's ball and then running for your life. But all of a sudden, we grow up, discover alcohol, start incrementally adding to the spare tyre around our midriff, desperately turn to running as a quick fix to deflate said tyre, then realise we don't actually know what we are doing. PE departments across the country are missing a trick if you ask me. Ever wondered why absolutely no one signs up for the 800m or 1500m on sports day? Yes, it is mildly more uncomfortable than jumping as far as you can into a sandpit and requires significantly more effort in comparison to a 20-second 100-metre race. But also, no kid knows what to do in those distances and how to take them on! We weren't taught how to pace one, or deal with the burn in your lungs when you still have one lap to the finish. Before you know it, somewhere along the line, you begin berating your old school teachers as you sign up for a half marathon during your mid-life crisis, wish you'd have put some effort in to cross country and wonder what the hell you have done after doing only 2 training runs.

Running is also considerably bullied by team sports throughout most individual's school career. Saturday mornings are very precious to 11-16-year-olds. So, making the choice between spending it in isolation pounding the streets chasing a 10k PB or jumping on the banter bus with all your mates battling it out for 90 minutes on a football pitch is a bit of a no brainer. The solitude that running often provides is not craved for by a young, sociable 15-year-old who wants the adrenaline rush of a crunching tackle or undeniable buzz of scoring the winner for their team. That same solitude becomes almost addictive to the full-time working parent with 2 young kids, a dog and a spouse who often struggles to defecate in peace let alone exercise. Getting up at 5am just to get their 30 minutes of peace from a morning run becomes a welcome necessity for the majority of middle-aged runners, not a chore. The accessibility and ease of running become so much more attractive the more and more life dumps responsibility on your shoulders. Just as much as the potential of that crunching Saturday morning tackle putting you out of work for 6 weeks also becomes less appealing as the years tick by.

Somehow, (I'm sure through some sort of trickery or bribery) we had a solid 6 turn out for the first Cross Country Club run on that famous Friday lunchtime. We couldn't have covered more than about a mile and a half in total, but my slightly tubby 8-year-old face was soon infused with a flourishing shade of deep purple and the ability to breathe seemed to elude me. Perhaps my peers had the right idea, all remaining in the relative safety of the concrete football pitch. Never the less, although my plum-resembling face didn't quite portray the same idea, I had enjoyed myself. And Mr Guite can take all the plaudits of where my love of running began. I can quite proudly say I did not miss any Friday lunchtime Cross Country Club runs from its inception in Year 3, until I concluded my primary school journey in Year 6. I built my way up just like you do on the seats of the school bus. At the beginning of your school career, you timidly place yourself as close to the exit as possible, unassumingly sitting down and keeping yourself to yourself. By year 6, you are reclining across the back seats, engraving your initials in the metal headrests and chanting every explicit school rhyme you know off by heart. I did the same with Cross Country Club. To start, I plodded along at the back, concentrating on making sure my lungs didn't explode. Fast forward a few years and I basically thought I was Paula Radcliffe, commanding the younger runners and giving them tips on breathing and pacing. I'm surprised I didn't adorn myself with a running number and medal ceremony after each run. We would enter cross country tournaments as a school competing across a 2 or 3-mile woodland run against the other local schools in the area. Don't get me wrong, I was by no means ever bringing home first place. But the unrivalled adrenaline rush of huddling together in our skin-tight white polo shirts and dishevelled trainers at the start line, nervously waiting for the gun, combined with the gutsy sprint finish drenched in mud and sweat at the end was nothing short of addictive. By the age of 11, I was craving those finish lines again and again.

I didn't just wait for Friday lunchtime; even from the age of about 8 onwards, I'd start little running trips of my own. Any reason to get out of my childhood home was a good one, so to be doing something I actually enjoyed as well was just a bonus. Little laps around the local park, running home from school, running to my friend's house, any chance I got I would be running. Granted, a lot of the time I'd also resemble an abandoned dog, chasing a tattered, old football whilst running. But the running was what I loved; having a ball as a reward was again just the icing on the top of the 'carb-loaded' cake. Mr 'G' had ignited a burning passion for running (and the endless freedom of the outdoors in general) and all I wanted to do was add fuel to the fire burning inside me and I knew just the other 'G' to help me do that.

It was the 5th July 2012 and the whole country was alive with the pure excitement and anticipation of the 27th Olympic Games being held in little old London in a few weeks' time. For an (at the time)19-year-old who had pretended she was Kelly Holmes from the age of about 4, this was an unbelievably inspiring time. I'm convinced I would have had my place in the 4 x 100m relay, strutting around Queen Elizabeth Olympic Park had I not still been suffering at that point with the after-effects of being wiped out by a lorry. What I did have was the absolute honour of being chosen as 1 out of 8,000 inspirational individuals to be a torch-bearer in the Olympic Torch Relay; not quite the 4 x 100m relay I'd dreamed of but my Christ I took it. The process to be allocated this accolade involved presenting nominations for torch-bearers to a very strict board of judges from all areas of sport, culture and media. They were to sift through and whittle down nominations that could come from quite literally any individual within the expectant public. You can well imagine that every single man, woman and child wanted to have this honour bestowed on them so the nominations for torch-bearers flooded in, in their hundreds of thousands. The nominations included community heroes that had been running soup kitchens for years, young budding sports stars that had overcome horrific illnesses and injuries, sports coaches and staff who had been facilitating youngsters' dreams on cold, wet Saturday mornings for years on end, teachers, doctors, nurses, all sorts of breath-taking stories... then there was me. My very good friend Francesca had nominated me due to the 'Infectious positivity and remarkable attitude shown to get back playing football and inspiring others through sport, despite receiving life-changing injuries when being involved in a terrible car accident.' Fran had very nobly recommended me for the honour based on a lie – that at the time she had absolutely no idea about. When I found out about the nomination and that I'd actually been chosen to be a torch-bearer, I was totally honoured but felt a complete fraud. I very nearly came clean to both Fran and the London Olympics Organising committee to say,

'I'm beyond honoured, but the car accident story is a lie. The truth is, I gave up on myself and everyone around me and the devastating injuries were a result of a cowardly suicide attempt.'

There is nothing inspirational about that. The first port of call for some reliable life advice (the same port I'd been visiting for 19 years) was, of course, my other 'BIG G', my paternal grandfather. I felt like it was a complete farce if I were to carry the torch amongst these other people who acted as pillars of their community, who had

70

committed their life to inspiring others, who had truly changed people's lives and there I was essentially nominated on the basis of a lie. What I didn't acknowledge at the time was that the way I sustained the life-changing injuries was irrelevant. I had my grandad and his reliably accurate advice to reassure me of that.

"Laura, you could have got your injuries from falling out of a tree (it would have needed to be a bloody big tree), getting bitten by a shark (that was my go-to story) or anything else; that part doesn't matter. These people chose you because you represent an Olympian's spirit. Whether you see it or not, the way you have pieced yourself back together to even be able to kick a ball is remarkable, never mind pulling on an Ipswich shirt again. You *are* remarkable. Now, I've got an old broomstick in the shed; get it above your head and do a few laps of the garden to get some practice in."

It was little gems of advice like that, which I can still pretty much reel off word for word 8 years later, which made my grandad the most supportive, influential and adoring man in my life. I believe 'Mr-Git' and he would have been firm friends had the opportunity arisen.

I'd never seen that man looking as proud as when we soaked up the atmosphere in Southold that beautiful Thursday morning. I was proudly posing for photos in my bright white torch-bearer outfit and Grandad was tracking down every passer-by, pointing like a maniac, letting them all know that was his granddaughter in the special tracksuit. I had never seen the pier so full of life and full of people. It seemed as if the whole population of the little seaside town had tipped out onto the beach to mark the once in a lifetime occasion. My leg of the relay was through the beautiful village of Reydon, just on the outskirts of Southwold. I left my grandad and my 2 friends who had come to support me at Southwold pier as all torch-bearers had a team bus to drop us off at the relevant start locations. Luckily, I was one of the first drops on the route, as, of course, the initial topic of conversation was the reasons we had all been nominated. I gladly jumped off the bus before I had to make up some dramatic story about being bitten by a wayward shark. The streets of Reydon were no different to those of Southwold. They were lined with Mums, Dads, schoolchildren, teachers, binmen, members of parliament, teenagers, dogs, babies and everyone else who had used this momentous day as a very justified reason not to go to work. Even the local residential home had wheeled out all of its excited golden oldies who parked their wheelchairs right on the start line of my relay. I greeted them all and posed for pictures like some 5-minute flash in the pan. Being the first runner of the route, I had my torch lit for me (instead of having the flame passed from another bearer) in front of the hordes of people. The beautiful gold circles making up the unique design of the torch glistened in the sunshine, the amber flames licking each small hollow as they scorched and waved out of the top of the beautiful structure. The buggers don't tell you, you have to pay £200 to keep your own torch. But it looked so stunning, proudly burning that traditional Olympic flame, being held aloft above my head, there was no chance I wasn't taking it home with me. I set off with a huge convoy of vehicles and support runners alongside me. Police cars, estate cars emblazoned with London 2012 Olympic slogans, the Olympic bus, medical vehicles. For the 3 minutes it took me to plod through the 600-metre leg, I felt like the eyes of the world were watching me. My peripheral vision was consumed with hundreds of the miniature union jack flags being ferociously waved by schoolchildren and their teachers who had been patiently waiting along the route all morning. I spotted friends in the crowd waving up and down like adoring fans at a music concert. It wasn't just them, complete strangers who had researched the torch-bearers coming to their town were shouting my name and cheering for me. I kept looking up at the flames burning strong at the tip of my torch, doing my best to take in every second of the quite overwhelming experience. This was the Olympic moment I'd dreamt of as a child. Kelly Holmes would have run a marathon in the time it took me to complete my 600m leg but that didn't matter. I flung my arms around my grandad as soon as I saw him, my heart still pumping out of my chest, and eagerly showed him my torch. He was never much of a one for glowing compliments but that day, he couldn't have been any prouder and neither could I. I often wonder were it not for his sound advice whether I would have taken my place as a torch-bearer that day. I owe so much to him; the Olympic Torch experience was as much his as it was mine. That day represented just a very small handful of what I learned from that wonderful man who has contributed to who I am today.

When I think of my Grandad Ray and the generation of people he was brought up by, I have nothing but admiration and respect. Not only for them as individuals but also their no-nonsense approach to life, which was inevitably reflected in their attitude towards exercise. The people born and raised in 1940s–1950s Britain were cut from a different cloth, especially when it came to exercise; they did things differently. Physical activity was perceived by many as a precious form of transport, my Grandad included, and they were so grateful for it. Exercise wasn't a chore or something that needed to be scheduled on the family whiteboard on a busy Wednesday night after the kid's karate and maths club. He didn't need to pay extortionate monthly subscription fees to participate in small group training, circuit training or to have tailored nutrition and exercise programmes. He didn't need to meet up with his gym buddies at 6am because they had all made themselves accountable to each other over 'What's App' the night before. He didn't need to employ a bouncy, extrovert Personal Trainer to motivate him to move or lose weight on a screen or in person. Their simplicity of life meant that shared good levels of fitness almost came as an unconscious bi-product because of the way they lived and the necessity to survive physically and financially.

Ray would think absolutely nothing of cycling 7 miles to work on a 20-year-old bike, doing a 10-hour physical shift and then cycling home again. He wasn't clad with an aerodynamic helmet nor did he carry an energy gel for the journey home. If he got a puncture, he would have to walk the rest. He would be grateful for the fact he had a job and a mode of transport to get him there for that matter. He would battle sleet, snow, wind and rain every day of the year because he hadn't even allowed himself to think of the luxury of a car. You can guarantee you would never, ever hear a word of complaint from the man. He was relentlessly positive in any given situation. He was the most stoic and resilient man I'd ever know and yes, that was partly because of the habitat he was brought up in but also because of his incredible zest for life. There was always, always a positive and matter-of-fact outlook on any incident. Raining and cold outside? It's good for the garden and that will make you appreciate the fire even more when you're home. Tired? Get moving again, you'll soon distract yourself. Leg chopped off? Well, good job you've got another one. Lost your job? Check down the back of the sofa you might find it (his humour was also infectious). No possible positive to be derived from the day at all? We'll put that one down to a bad day and have a better one tomorrow. There was no self-pity, no entitlement and no excuses. It was his choice and his responsibility to establish this wonderfully commendable attitude and I completely admired him for it.

He would probably have porridge for breakfast, a sandwich for lunch and meat and vegetables for dinner. The vegetables more than likely came from an allotment that he would tend to for hours on a Sunday morning, burning far more calories completing the functional movements of digging, weeding and planting than losing the will to live battling with a cross-trainer that doesn't replicate any sort of natural movement in the slightest. Exercise wasn't an additional element to the routine; it was incorporated into every strand of life and was also a necessary requirement to be able to survive. Yes, of course, he had a factory football team that played in the league when they all clocked off at midday on a Saturday. But that was the only organised form of recreational activity they had and it was a pleasurable 90 minutes of entertainment out of a 55-hour working week.

When his dutiful wife went shopping, she didn't have 46 different varieties of crisps and cereal bars to choose from. They didn't have the new improved £16 custard cream with added protein and vitamins. It was a rare sight to see an overweight person in 1940's-1950's Britain and arguably, post-World War II food rationing contributed to that. But also, it was the combination of being genuinely grateful for what they had, not being able to give in to late-night gluttony because the food simply wasn't there (and if it was, it was a potato or stale bread) and embracing exercise as a way of life as opposed to a necessary evil to look good for others' validation. They didn't sit down to vegetate after inhaling as much Sunday dinner and dessert as possible to then fall asleep in front of the non-existent television. They would go for a long afternoon walk and actually, would you believe it, enjoy themselves. I truly believe if we were to adopt their attitude to exercise, work, and nutrition, the exercise industry would go bust. If we as a society now were made to go without our protein-infused custard creams and just receive the quantity of food we *needed* instead of the quantity we *wanted* – it would be one of the biggest weight-loss initiatives ever. Imagine if we were deprived of our cars or efficient public transport for a few weeks and had to rely on our own energy to get us to where we wanted to be.

My little Ray of sunshine was the embodiment of what it meant to be a grandparent and his appreciation of the capacity of the human body inevitably rubbed off on me. The impalpable excitement of a grandchild chasing their Grandad around the garden on a summer afternoon should be the foundation of every childhood. That man would never tire. He would never appear dejected, exasperated or even mildly jaded after a solid morning playing 7-a-side football. Throughout his senior years, he still got more of a workout messing around with his beloved grandchildren than his mates at over-seventies sit down fit exercise class. My Grandad epitomised the word inspiration and I couldn't wait to start employing his resolute attitude in every aspect of my life as soon as I was old enough to appreciate it.

The indomitable combination of Mr Guite and my grandad started my insatiable thirst for pushing the boundaries of physical exertion and I will forever be indebted to the both of them. Not only do I inherit my appetite for adventure from the 2 G's, but also the associated unflappable, stoic attitude needed to accomplish such feats whilst quivering on the edge of your comfort zone. I wish that they had both met one another; they would have been as thick as thieves. I can just imagine them both now heading out on a long early-morning walk. They would both be immaculately equipped for the conditions and already discussing the fresh morning air and how many miles they were going to cover, eagerness and energy positively radiating from the pair of them. Following a solid 10-mile hike, I can guarantee they would wash up and wear nearly the exact same chequered shirt in the pub for a few well-deserved pints afterwards.

Watching the man, whom I had always known to be so effervescent and so utterly brimming with life, suddenly succumb to illness was inexplicably heart-breaking. The last few years of his life were riddled with different, debilitating illnesses that culminated in the re-growth of a previously partly removed brain tumour. As expected, throughout the majority of his illness he remained unbelievably upbeat. There were countless days and nights where he would be in a significant amount of pain but would, without fail, muster a smile and still smash through a long-anticipated breakfast or evening meal. We would spend a matter of seconds discussing the physical problems that he was facing, before he was far more interested in what I was doing or the next challenge I was pursuing. He was the most selfless, conscientious human being on the planet.

I recall a much-cherished memory from when Grandad was in hospital for a prostate operation. He had spent most of the morning telling me all about a completely gorgeous nurse that was looking after him and how he was charming her into giving him extra biscuits with his tea. The nurse in question came striding into her ward like a modern-day Florence Nightingale, beaming as she approached my grandad, whose irresistible charm had clearly worked its magic on her already.

"Hello, Ray, how are you today?"

Before the dot had barely been placed on the bottom of her question mark, he was gleefully replying,

"Cerys, this is my granddaughter, Laura; she runs marathons!"

The imperative medical information that the lovely nurse was trying to convey to that old man was falling on completely deaf ears as he kept eagerly interrupting with stories of our football matches or listing my achievements to her like some sort of award ceremony. He was so completely desperate to share his pride with someone else it just melted my heart. When Cerys the nurse had finally finished, he would be back to fulfilling the needs of his mischievous streak almost immediately. Cerys began helping him fill out a feedback form for the ward. And of course, being 2018 at the time, it wouldn't take long for this question to crop up,

"Raymond, could you firstly let me know how you would describe your sexual orientation?"

Grandad slowly looked over at me and I just knew he was concocting some witty but well-mannered response.

"I'm a lesbian, Cerys!"

As much as Cerys was trying to uphold the strictest of professional standards, my granddad's harmless mischief and infectious smile couldn't help but illuminate the day of anyone whose company he shared. And I could see Cerys trying to hold back a wry smile as she noted down his rather inaccurate answer. As you can imagine, the rest of the feedback form provided the whole ward with a rather colourful 20 minutes and, as I was accustomed to, anyone within reaching distance of my grandad now had a much brighter smile than they did before being in his presence.

His tumour began to engulf his entire brain and with that, his stunning personality began to drain out of him hour by hour, along with his characteristic humour. But there was absolutely nothing we could do. The radiance that he would bring to every room he strolled into faded as he lost the ability to walk. The way he would captivate any and every audience with his hilarious adventures of yonder years merged into a sad silence as a state of bewilderment and unease dominated his entire outlook. The warm and affectionate cuddle that would embrace you through triumph and turmoil changed hands, as his need for love and reassurance was far greater than mine. The impeccable gentleman that my grandad was and the standards he withheld were displayed in even his most desperate days. I cannot begin to imagine the sheer terror a person must go through when being governed by an unstoppable growth which impacts on every inch of one's personality, psychological function and decision-making. I cannot begin to fathom what he must have experienced being overwhelmed by a tumour that steals every ounce of your being and doesn't even allow you to know what day it is. But even when dealing with that unimaginable disorientation, he was the epitome of grace and dignity. Through the humiliation he was suffering, he always managed a please and a thank you. He always put out a hand to greet you. He was never aggressive or rude and the beautiful blue of his eyes didn't fade, not until the very last moment. I was so overwhelmingly proud of that man in every way possible, but even more so, in the way he dealt with those last few months. I make it my mission every single day to bring just as much happiness to other people as he did to all those around him.

We lost my grandad on the 18th of March 2020, just a month before we were scheduled to go ahead with the initial 10-10-10 start date and a mere 5 days before the nationwide lockdown order commenced in this country. Given the state of his psychological condition in the days and weeks leading up to his death, I had no expectation of him understanding what I was trying to achieve with my most recently planned running endeavour, but I still told him and spoke to him about it in the most intricate detail. I strongly believed that some of it was still going in. Even if my running waffle provided him with some slight comfort, even if just by hearing the recognisable tone of my voice, it was worth doing. I would still sit and talk to him for ages in his sleep. Usually, he would always be the first port of call when undertaking a new challenge. His candid and honest reactions to my plentiful ideas (his facial expression would be all I needed to know what he was thinking) would always help me to gauge how doable it was, whatever it may have been, and also how ridiculous it was. His belief in me never wavered. I could have told him I was bunny-hopping to Malaysia with a washing machine on my back and he would still have entire faith that I could complete it. However, he would also hold his very private reservations about my health and welfare very close to his chest and only voice them in the most diplomatic and necessary fashion. His memory for, not just mine, but all of his grandchildren's achievements was quite astounding. He'd still reel off cup final scores from years ago or pluck out the name of a teacher or friend, seemingly out of thin air, that must have only been mentioned to him a handful of times. The culmination of all of his utterly charming qualities and the striking ability of that man to not only be the most heart-warming grandparent but also my reliable best friend, meant that the pain caused by losing him was far greater than running any marathon.

His passing was imminent and I had known it could have been arriving any day for weeks, but the morning I received the call it still didn't register at all. Being the personality that I am, my first focus had to be that he'd had a solid innings, was comfortable and surrounded by family when he died and most importantly, he gave unreserved joy to every person he came in to contact with throughout his life. Unfortunately, that didn't detract from losing him at a time when the world wasn't allowing you to grieve properly in the most unprecedented pandemic my generation and the one before me had ever experienced. The man would have filled any establishment with hundreds of people had we been allowed a 'normal' funeral service. The place would have been bursting at the seams with friends, family, neighbours, checkout operators, dog-walkers, builders and shop owners; just about anyone he had come across and adopted as a friend the minute they met. But the Government restrictions because of Covid-19 allowed us just 10 people at his funeral. 10. We were not allowed to hug. We were not allowed to physically comfort or reassure the people we loved who were visibly suffering. We had to sit 2 metres apart from one another and the place where we were conducting his send-off felt and looked just as empty as my heart. We were most certainly not the first or last family to partake in a 'Lockdown funeral' but it provided no closure on such sadness at all. The traditional wake, in which my grandad would have taken great pleasure in looking down on everyone having one too many sherbets, whilst reminiscing about his adventures, simply could not go ahead. Yet again, as with so many extraordinary periods of history, which the Covid-19 pandemic would undoubtedly be classed as, we all learn from it and took away our individual lessons. The world will never again take for granted a full funeral or the privilege of inviting whoever you so wish. We will now forever relish the opportunity to embrace one another to soften the blow of the overwhelming grief. Moving forward, we will all now collectively interpret death differently and hopefully have a greater recognition of the processes providing closure on life's ultimate inevitability.

Chapter 4.

Ironlady

The male-dominated aura of one of the world's greatest endurance events is epitomised by the name IRONMAN. For centuries, females have been underestimated, protected, patronized, condescended. Not just in physical competition but from the very onset of human existence. Our Neanderthal Ancestors were the first example of this; they left manual labour and physical endurance to the male side of the family;

"No, no you stay in the cave, love, I'll go out and kill the wild animal to put on the fire – you stay here and comb the lice out of your hair."

Throughout history, it is only when women have *had* to step up to the physical exertion plate, that they have displayed our tenacious adaptability to excel at whatever is expected of us.

Lily Parr (26th April 1905 – 24th May 1978) was a stunning example of a woman who excelled in her sport – but it was only when a world war broke out, that was she given the opportunity to display it. As WW1 broke out in 1914, male-dominated work pursuits and recreational activities had to be adopted by women because there were simply not enough men on home turf to complete them. Parr was a talented footballer as a child and honed her craft playing with her older brothers on wastelands near her home of St Helens. She later worked for the Preston Munitions factory, more commonly known as Dick, Kerr & Co and reportedly earned 10 shillings (along with her teammates) in expenses per game. Essentially, female football teams became professional and were paid to play the game throughout the war years whilst attracting crowds of up to 50,000 spectators. The normal male game that would attract the hordes couldn't be played as there were no blokes on home soil to play it. This would strongly suggest to me that the female teams played good quality football and entertained the crowds just as successfully as their male counterparts. Otherwise, why would 50,000 people find precious spare money to go and watch them? The male-dominated sport had only been male-dominated because women were not given the chance to play.

Shockingly, when WW1 was over, it didn't take the Football Association long to quickly rip the heart out of the then-well-established female game and the idea that the general public were ever supportive of it. In 1921, the British FA banned all women from playing on their member grounds in a gut-wrenchingly deceptive tactic to ensure women could no longer play competitively. Female footballers of the WW1 era were picked up, used, exploited and then monumentally dropped when all the blokes returned home as heroes. And quite rightly they should return as heroes. But the heroines that had been gracing the pitch every week whilst they were away, had been entirely shunned. Yes, the men were away experiencing atrocities no man or woman should ever see, hear or feel. But, the female athletes of the time were maintaining fitness whilst working manual labour jobs, looking after the home and their children and preserving some well-needed morale by entertaining thousands every week with their sporting skill and talent. Instead of proudly being awarded heroine status throughout this harrowing period, they were silenced, ignored, forgotten. Just imagine the impact it would have had to female sport today had the professional female game (and the progressive momentum it had gathered) been allowed to continue and develop back in 1921. Could that have been the shift required to elevate women to the level they deserved to be at in professional sport at the turn of the century? If the women of the 1900s had sufficient training, exposure and approval in just one sport, maybe, just maybe, it would have changed the way we view women's sport today.

The first person to break a 4-minute mile? Male. The first person to swim the Channel? Male. The first person to cycle the length of the UK? Male. The Olympics had been established for 4 years before women were even allowed to compete. The first-ever Olympic Games held in 1896 had only male competitors. And even when women were 'allowed' their opportunity to compete, it was only in sports, 'Compatible with their femininity and fragility. 'It wasn't until 1928 that women were allowed to compete in athletics and gymnastics events. Unbelievably, it wasn't until 2012 that women's boxing was finally added to the Olympic schedule, therefore, meaning that every Olympic sport had both a male and female competition but it took nearly 100 years to do so.

The 1967 Boston Marathon is arguably more famous for the fact Kathrine Switzer, despite being an officially registered competitor, was manhandled throughout her run by the race director, Jock Semple, in an attempt to prevent her from competing. Switzer completed the race, but because of her pioneering efforts, women were then banned following her participation (here we go again) from competing with men. It wasn't until 5 years later in 1972 that the Boston Marathon established an Official Women's Race. Another prominent example of women's talent, ability and potential being thwarted, because they had the audacity to place themselves on an equal standing with male athletes. This was combined with the clear fact that chauvinistic male race directors of the time couldn't handle a powerful woman just wanting to run. And not just run, actually 'outrun' a good percentage of male competitors on the course.

Was this common attitude born out of the idea that women were not biologically capable at the time of achieving what a man could? Potentially. Is it because women weren't willing to commit to training as hard as a man could? I don't think so. Is this because women didn't want to? Absolutely not. The point I'm trying to illustrate here is that the reason the first person to win a marathon, swim the channel or cycle the length of the country was male, or that one of the most well-known endurance events in the world is named IRONMAN, is down to opportunity. Even now, we are still on occasion battling against the prehistoric ideology that even allowing a woman to compete in some sports is classed as preposterous.

Only in 2012 in London did Saudi Arabia have their first-ever female Olympian, Sarah Attar, who competed in the 800m. Attar will now remain as a female trailblazer in her respective country. Despite the accolade of becoming an Olympian for Saudi Arabia and it being the 21st century, not the Middle Ages, she was still expected to wear running clothing compliant with Islamic Law (perfect for sweltering summertime running). It was reported at the time that 'escaped' images of her running in completely appropriate running clothing (shorts and T-shirt- how daringly explicit and revealing of her...) were deleted from the internet like some sort of disgusting sexual act. Yet again, the country's honour, reputation and a female conforming to the age-old parameters set for her by law, is far more important than those crucial few milliseconds which decent running attire can grab you. Imagine in 1954 if a *woman* was exposed to exactly the same training programme as Sir Roger Bannister, had exactly the same amount of time to dedicate to their craft, the exact same team around them focusing on the same goal. Could the first-ever sub-4-minute mile have been run by a woman? Realistically, we will never know. What I do know, is ask most mediocre pub teams to name 3 male Tour De France winners and 3 male London Marathon winners and they wouldn't struggle. Change the question to female winners,(other than Paula Radcliffe) and I guarantee they'd struggle to get 1 and a half.

However, when progression does occur, when we do stumble across an incredibly talented, prolific female athlete in the form of South African 800m runner Caster Semenya, she is ostracized for being too masculine! Because a country like South Africa needs an excuse to ostracize. Obviously, a woman couldn't possibly be successful due to talent, hard work, structured training or relentless commitment. It must be because she is illegally modifying herself to become more like a man. It was a quite momentous occasion in 2010 when the International Association of Athletics (IAAF) who had previously suspended her from International competition for 'sex testing', cleared her to return to competing, because, guess what? They found nothing illegal within her private or training regime. Her hormone levels were within the accepted levels expected of a female athlete. The fact we need to adhere to strict hormone levels in competitive sport says a lot about the narrowing male/female divide within it. Yet it also suggests there is still doubt over whether a female may be able to compete at the same standard as a man. Yes, you'd not be human if you didn't double-take at Semenya's exceptionally defined biceps, rippling abdominal muscles and chiselled jawline, but does this make her any less of a woman? No. Her strikingly athletic, powerful physique makes her even more of a female warrior if you ask me.

I'd forgive you for thinking I'm a feminist. I'm not. I get just as infuriated as anyone else when Veronica Ramsbottom and her Women's Institute cronies think their shit doesn't stink, simply because they have ovaries. I do not believe women are better than anyone. I do not believe they are entitled to more. I believe they are equal and deserve every opportunity to give a good account of themselves – especially when it comes to sport, running and endurance events in general. I adamantly disagree that the Women's Wimbledon Champion should be paid the same as the Male Wimbledon Champion if she has consistently played for 3 sets throughout the tournament, as opposed to the male expectation of 5 sets. Some female matches between a top 5 ranked seed and some enthusiastic outsider ranked 145th in the world can last no longer than 45 minutes. Whereas, the potential 5-set super slog of a male encounter could last for hours. Either the LTA makes the male and female competition run for the same amount of sets, or pay your competitors accordingly based on the amount of time they have been playing, or working, as it were. However, you only have to momentarily look at the back of any popular newspaper spanning the past 20 years to see how completely male-dominated sports reporting is in the media. The male national football team need to beat San Marino 1-0 in the qualifying stages of a World Cup and they get a detailed, 4-page spread on every back page in the country, including analysis of patterns of play, statistics and an in-depth discussion on each player's contribution to the victory. Hell, they will probably even throw in a sticker book and free stickers if they reach the quarter-finals. The female national football team need to reach the semi-final of a major, worldwide competition, blindfolded, walking on their hands and singing the national anthem backwards before getting so much as a paragraph next to the horse racing results. I'm being facetious but you get my point. Annoyingly, it's almost as though our culture has become accustomed to it. We just accept the fact male sport gets more coverage in the media because, supposedly, that's just the way the world works. It shouldn't just be a matter of time passing and the world becoming less discriminatory for women to get the broadcasting they deserve. However, it does feel to me as if we are making some steady progress. We now have regular female punditry across the board on national television, female commentators, female officials and proud female athletes becoming household names. Before you know it, the Friday night television staple may get even better should we get a female team captain on' A Question of Sport'.

Understandably, when I first began to learn that one of the most gruelling endurance events out there was colloquially known as an IRONMAN, of course I was going to attempt it. Along with (at last) a satisfyingly gender-balanced field of other athletes. I'm not belittling the skill, stamina or endurance level of any type of sport. However, the current male world record holder for an

IRONMAN distance triathlon (at the time of writing in June 2020) is Jan Frodeno of Germany. He completed the 2.4-mile swim, 112-mile bike ride and 26.2-mile run in a staggering time of 7 hours 51 minutes and 13 seconds. Just let that sink in for a moment. When you consider it can take some people 6 hours to complete just the marathon discipline, that time is absolutely mind-blowing. I guarantee you a significant amount of readers devouring this book (hopefully without falling asleep) will have never, ever heard of Jan Frodeno, but could name, for example, 5 or 6 international snooker players. Now, snooker is a highly-skilled, tactical and psychologically demanding pursuit. But there is absolutely no way any snooker player has had to dig so deep into their mental and physical reserves for that last 6-mile torture of an Ironman marathon. They have never really had to grit their teeth, get their head down, ignore the searing pain screaming through their legs and lungs, (both begging them to stop) or carry on and get the job done. They have never had to physically suffer for their sport. I'm taking nothing away from snooker. I'm just trying to illustrate that we just don't give enough acclaim and acknowledgement to endurance sports and the athletes that diligently train for them to then give their absolute life and soul when competing.

You so much as mention the phrase 'IRONWOMAN/LADY' and if your next word isn't 'MAGGIE' or 'THATCHER', you are met with a cloud of confusion. But, of course, an endurance event consisting of a 2.4-mile open water swim, 112-mile bike ride and a

26.2-mile run couldn't possibly be named after a female because, quite simply, only women would enter. It would be entirely emasculating to some men, not all, to put themselves through the torment of months of hard training, commitment and sacrifice to then finally slog out a 16-hour day, to end up with a title denoting female attributes. Call it an IRONMAN, however, and any woman will jump at the chance of entering, irrelevant of the disproportionate amount of men they are competing against, or what gender their achievement may be called at the finish. Or, prepare yourself, *deep inhale*, that they may even have the potential to be faster than any other bloke competing.

I loved the appeal of an 'IRONMAN.' Coming from a background of football, (the most working-class sport going) the idea of strutting around with middle-class men and women, parading their £10,000 bikes with diamond-encrusted spokes like racehorses at Aintree, was both entertaining and exciting. I know I have always had, as the saying goes, 'an old head on young shoulders', but you'd certainly be excused if you mistakenly pronounced TRI-ATH-LON as MID-LIFE-CRISIS. At every new event I experienced, I seemed to be uncomfortably sandwiched between a 54-year-old CEO from Devon with more money than sense, in a £600 wetsuit, and his best mate who had only retired 18 months ago, but was already getting on his wife's tits so decided to take up a sport that would consume at least 60% of his time. With the additional potential to consume up to 65% of his week if you take into account training, third spare bike shopping, having a beer with fellow triathlon 'wankers' after a Sunday long ride and talking incessantly about running split times. I, however, did not have a spare £600, any triathlon wanker friends or the disposable income to have a spare inner tube, let alone a spare bike, nor did I have an irritable wife at home. Just a desire, from the age of about 11, to push the boundaries of physical endurance.

When you consider that running marathons barefoot has been an exponentially increasing trend for a good few years now; it's debatable that a £500 pair of trainers will have little to no impact on your marathon PB. Also, take into consideration that the first woman to swim the Channel in 1926, Gertrude Ederle, wore a self-made swimsuit, made with any material she could lay her hands on, covered in cooking grease; there is not much argument for a £1000 wetsuit making an impact on your performance. The same, unfortunately, can't be said for owning a road bike. Five grand can make a significant dent in your timings whilst chasing down the road miles. Be it an aluminium frame, aerodynamic handlebars or a bloody engine on the back of it, put it this way, money talks when it comes to Triathlon and they are all necessary purchases. But that didn't matter to me; swimming, cycling and running were just the purest of sports in my opinion. They were the foundation of your childhood – or at least they should have been. Think about it. When you were gleefully chasing round the school field playing 'IT' or 'Stuck in the Mud' or you were chasing your mate on your BMX playing cops and robbers and your heart was pounding out of your chest, you never once bent down, clutched both your knees and said,

"Jesus, I'm not as fit as I thought." Or, "I'm getting too old for this."

You were just overcome with excitement at freeing your mate from their mud-stricken stance or finding the nasty robbers in the bushes. You were free, you were alive, a bit wild and a bit untamed but you didn't have a care in the world. Arguably, the 'not a care in the world' bit comes from being 8 years old and having very little stress, worries or responsibility. But at 8 years old, I had already had my fair share of life experience and even then, albeit unconsciously, exercise was my escape. I suppose I am one of the lucky ones, because that freedom, that physical expression and carefree existence that running or cycling or swimming facilitates for you, transferred straight from childhood into adulthood without a single glitch. I'm still at my happiest in a pair of trainers, on a bike, in a lake or playing stuck in the mud. I have learned, however, that a game of stuck in the mud amongst fully grown adults is frustratingly deemed as slightly less socially acceptable. But, if you pretend you are either intoxicated or part of a hen do, then it's absolutely fine.

Outlaw triathlon was due to take place on July 28th 2019 at Nottingham Water Sports Centre, a beautiful setting that had been fully adorned, everywhere you looked, with the well-known bright orange colour of the Outlaw brand. It was like walking into a giant can of

Fanta. The great big can of orange pop was buzzing with indisputable 'triathlon wankers' discussing tyre width, wetsuit buoyancy and gravity-defying shoelaces. I really wasn't qualified enough to participate in these conversations, so I just smiled at them to reciprocate our shared enthusiasm for human endeavour. With my partner faithfully by my side, we registered, filled our bags to the brim with freebies, strolled around and got pestered by vegan energy gel companies and set the tent up for the night. All there was left to do was keep eating until we burst (with maybe a couple of free vegan energy gels for good measure) and get ready to jump in the reservoir at 6am the following morning.

I was preparing for it to be an unforgettable Sunday, where the 3 purest sport forms all come together and give each other a great big cuddle, in a 16-hour display of positivity, psychological resilience and physical achievement. But Outlaw 2019 had a slightly different plan for me and all the other wannabe Ironmen (and women). Throughout the Saturday night, I had packed and repacked my bag at least 14 times and laid out my running gear next to thousands of others in the expansive white marquee, that had a distinct smell of school PE changing rooms. My swim hat had been dusted liberally with talcum powder and my neck smothered in Vaseline, like a well-greased turkey ready to roast. My tri-suit was adjusted to within an inch of its life leaving absolutely nothing to the imagination. Energy bars and gels had been forced into every spare orifice going (in both my body and my bike) and Percy the bike had been pumped up and safely racked alongside plenty of other 2-wheeled friends for the night. The 2.4-mile open water swim, 112-mile bike ride and 26.2-mile run that awaited me in the morning was still mildly terrifying but I could not be any more prepared.

The swim start was everything I imagined it would be. After a goosebump-inducing countdown, the starting claxon sounded and a completely chaotic, breathless concoction of arms, elbows and legs ensued, all simultaneously clambering through murky water trying to get an uninterrupted stroke in. Just as I regained my breath after the cold water had unashamedly filled my nostrils, eardrums and eyeballs to the brim, I was struggling for it again after I had been dunked by yet another scrambling swimmer. After a couple of kicks in the ribs and the odd elbow to the cheek (both bodily variations), the vast array of swimming ability at such an event became very noticeable as the pack started to disperse. Some competitors would be finishing the 2.4 miles in 45 minutes, others in 1 hour 45 minutes. Stroke after stroke, breath after breath, like a well-oiled machine, I found my rhythm. Other than a couple of close encounters with the large buoys (as a proud gay woman I'm not that accustomed to encounters with boys of any kind), the months of training paid off and the 2.4 miles soon flew by. I was gladly assisted out of the water by the hardy volunteers who had been submerged to waist height for at least 2 hours, hauling every single wobbly swimmer out of the reservoir by their wrinkled wrists and taking quite a lot of pleasure in it by the looks of things. As soon as I was on dry land, I was emphatic. I felt confident and powerful and couldn't wait to get on 2 wheels. That was 1 out of 3 disciplines complete. When you consider a full IRONMAN day can take anything up to 17 hours, the couple of hours it took me to splash around the lake didn't quite feel like a third of the way there, but I'd made a cracking start. But the dry land was unusually crowded and there was a very uncertain atmosphere lingering in the dank air. Surely there shouldn't be this many bikes still here? I'm no slouch but I'm also no Michael Phelps; there must be more people that have swum quicker than I have? I knew it had been raining for most of the night. The gentle pitter-patter of the droplets bouncing off our tent canvas was quite soothing to my over-stimulated brain in the early hours preceding the day's events. But apparently, the heavens had opened and dumped an absolute skinful whilst we were in the water. Understandably, when you are open-water swimming, you really don't notice the rain that much. A bit like being caught in a hurricane and someone asking you if you had noticed the wind picking up. A marshal soon gave an explanation as to why there were so many Triathletes expectantly waiting around looking rather dejected.

"THE BIKE ROUTE IS FLOODED. WATER HAS COMPLETELY SUBMERGED THE ROAD. THERE WILL BE NO BIKE SECTION OF OUTLAW TRIATHLON. THE BIKE SECTION IS CANCELLED. PLEASE AWAIT YOUR MARATHON RUN START TIME."

'No. No. No. No. No. NO! That cannot be possible. It was a light drizzle, not a monsoon. There has been some sort of mistake. We can avoid the puddles, can't we? We can just get off and walk through them?' No, we couldn't. The torrential downpour had left sections of the route completely flooded, not even safe for a car to drive through, never mind a bike. They weren't puddles, they were more like small streams. Astonishingly quickly, I went from emphatic to completely desolate. I had plunged into a state of disbelief and despair. This brilliant, time-consuming, energy-sapping, financially draining little dream I'd been working on for 7 months was now crumbling in front of my eyes. That will probably sound completely overdramatic to someone who has never trained for an endurance event before. But to me, this project had consumed everything associated with my life, my thoughts, my concerns, my spare time, my social life, my sleep, my diet, my bank account and the majority of my conversations for 7 months and I was now expected to run a marathon knowing full well that even after a 26.2-mile slog, I wasn't going to achieve what I set out to and what I so desperately wanted to. It would still only be 2 out of 3 of the disciplines completed. It was as if I had run 25 miles of another marathon and all of sudden the organisers pulled the plug and decided not to let you complete it.

Many competitors just started packing up and going home. I watched them as they despondently collected their pristinely serviced and cleaned bike and running trainers and started the lonely walk back to the campsite.

An eerie silence engulfed Nottingham Water Sports Centre, only intermittently broken by the announcer letting competitors know any updates. It took every fibre of my being not to succumb to just packing up and going home. These people (who themselves had spent months getting this event organised for us all) were giving me the opportunity to run a marathon, despite the fact, at the time, it meant nothing to me. I could have run 100 miles that afternoon but I still wouldn't have been an IRONMAN. It was an appropriate time to rely on the old life experience and find some perspective and pride from somewhere, anywhere I could. You haven't just had your leg bitten off by a lost shark in the 2.4-mile swim. You haven't been deprived of the opportunity of completing an IRONMAN for the next 40 years of your life. You haven't just lost the ability to function. Get a bit of pride about you, Laura, get your head out of your arse, go and do what you know you can do and use this experience to build you.

It turned out to be the hardest marathon I would ever run. I had no purpose. I had no motivation to finish. It was the first time in my life where finishing a marathon would literally have no positive impact on my psychological well-being. So much motivation to finish a marathon, or any endurance-based feat for that matter, is derived from the electrifying, breath-taking experience at the finish line. The imminent 5 hours of running around Nottingham would be one of the greatest tests of mental resilience I'd ever experienced. This just wasn't the same as every other apprehensive start line I'd stood upon.

What an earth was going to drive me through the pain barrier at mile 20, still with an hour of running to go, when I knew in my heart, I would just be numb at the end? I wasn't excited to finish. I wasn't bothered by what the medal was going to feel like. I couldn't join in with the conventional start-line banter. But I forced my dampened spirit (literally and metaphorically as it had started to teem it down again) to be thankful for the opportunity, ability and privilege to run and started to put one foot in front of the other.

The silky, nylon material of my favourite running top had become sodden and was clinging to my skin. Every bump and groove of my torso could be followed by the pattern formed by my soaking wet top. My trainers had doubled in weight from the rain as they squelched through every one of the 43,000 steps I was taking around Nottingham. Yet, the cognitive power created in oneself through running soon transformed my disgusting mood into a mildly positive focus, to finish what had been put in front of me at the very least. The goalposts had changed. Yes, this was not what I had set out to achieve and I was bitterly disappointed that I would not become an IRONMAN on that day. However, the methodical plodding of one step after another ironically managed to transform any negative into a positive; even if the negative is, in fact, the running event itself!

'Around the lake, out and back. Around the lake, out and back.'

I was repeating the race brief and course to myself in my head just to have something to focus on. The course comprised of 3 laps of the lake we had swum in that very morning and an out and back route taking in the local sights of Nottingham Town. We could have been circling Buckingham Palace or doing every step in the car park, it wouldn't have made any difference to me. Eventually, I got to the finish line that was so professionally constructed, beautifully adorned with congratulatory messages and emblazoned with the recognisable, bright orange 'Outlaw' emblem; I felt totally unworthy running underneath it. I didn't even clock my time, which I would normally do after every single run. I looked at the poor volunteer handing me my medal like she was hanging a dirty nappy around my neck. I fell into my partner's arms and just cried. I'd just completed my first ever 2.4-mile open water swim and run my 5th marathon, but I was empty. That self-dictatorial, self-critical, belittling personality that I'd been battling with for 26 years cast its curse again. What I had achieved wasn't good enough. What I had achieved was a world away from what it should have been. It was nowhere near good enough. Only 1% of the population has run 1 marathon let alone 5 and I guarantee that the percentage of the country who have swum 2.4 miles in open water is even less than that. But that was irrelevant. The fact that the reason I couldn't become an IRONWOMAN that day was due to an external variable – entirely out of my control - was also irrelevant. I would berate myself for at least 3 days for failing to reach my goal. I'd selfishly and belligerently refuse to find any positive in the 2/3rds of an IRONMAN distance triathlon I had completed. That negative bubble I myself had put around my world was momentarily burst with a purposeful finger when I was quickly made aware of the little- known event called the 'MIDNIGHT (WO)MAN TRIATHLON.'

Exactly 2 weeks from the date of my first failed IRONMAN attempt, another organised, competitive Ironman-distance Triathlon was due to take place, in Dartford, starting off with the swim section at 6pm and taking place throughout the night. I had never even heard of Midnight Man but this was an absolute no brainer, wasn't it? I didn't need any convincing at all but the inclusive 'WO' in brackets in the title all over the website and merchandise was the confidence boost I needed. I filled out the registration form, drained the life out of my overdraft (if an overdraft isn't for a second attempt in 2 weeks at an IRONMAN triathlon, then what is it for?) and clicked that confirm button without even blinking. It gradually started to feel like I was kicking that overbearing monkey off my shoulder. Midnight Man was at the complete opposite end of the spectrum to Outlaw in terms of publicity and recognition in the triathlon community. Outlaw was the glamorous, high-end event, littered with nutrition freebies, vivacious supporters and marketing and advertising campaigns. It was plastered all over social media and anyone within a 5-mile radius of a triathlon wanker would have probably heard of it. Midnight Man was a 400-participant event, organised and facilitated by one brilliant60ish-year-old triathlon veteran, pretty much on his own, with 12 and a half supporters and a couple of custard creams and bags of ready salted at the feed stations. Whether there were 3 people at the finish or 300, or whether there were scientific electrolyte tablets at the feed station or a solitary orange segment, all that mattered to me was that they covered exactly the same distance and represented the same enormous achievement.

Of course, the weather was dubious for the second attempt too. I looked out onto the choppy lake as the water crashed into the buoys and thought how reminiscent the lake was of my uneasy stomach. The gusts of wind were due to die down throughout the night, so at least I'd only have to swallow a gut load of river water in the windy conditions and not have too much of a battle against it head-on, on 2 wheels or 2 feet. The choppy conditions delivered exactly as expected and within the first 400 metres, I was lapping up lake water like a Labrador on a summer's afternoon. The 4-lap route of the lake took you directly into the path of the setting sun, which was both beautiful and blinding at exactly the same time. My (already poor) navigational ability in open water was being momentarily scuppered by the setting sun over Dartford. This combined with my steamed up, non-reflective goggles made the 2.4-mile swim slightly more wayward than it should have been, but with a gentle nudge in the right direction from the supporting kayaks, I got it done in a respectable time of 1 hour 40 minutes.

I was just waiting for a race organiser to inform me King Kong had descended on the bike route, causing man-sized potholes, or it had started inexplicably snowing in the middle of August. I was convinced another unforeseen, ludicrous, external variable would impact on my IRONMAN dream again and cancel the bike discipline. Thankfully, it was seasonably warm and King Kong decided to stay home that evening and I jumped on Percy the bike so quickly, the world didn't have the chance to throw a curveball in again.

The bike route, most importantly, was dry but also made up of laps. 26 laps of a 4.3-mile route made up the 112 miles I needed to cover, which initially didn't seem that intimidating. I was ticking off the laps both in my head and verbally to break the midnight silence, chipping away at it, 20 to go, 15 to go and so on. For the purposes of the book, I would have loved the cycle route to have been through undulating hills, picturesque countryside with new-born lambs to the left and quaint village cottages to the right. Elderly residents hanging out their laundry on 50-year-old rotary washing lines, in pristinely kept gardens, waving as you glide on by. Well, let me tell you now, it wasn't. It was 112 miles of dual carriageway, tarmac and beige residential estates in the pitch-black hours of the night with the odd frantic squirrel chucked in for a little bit of excitement. It was a good job I didn't care for quaint country villages; I was just so relieved the notorious second discipline was being completed.

After 112 miles and 7.5 hours on a bike, I was actually craving the motion of putting one foot in front of the other to provide some light relief to my astonishingly sore arse. The slight discomfort I was in after nearly 9 hours of physical activity at that point was so welcome. That is what I thrive off. Tired? Legs burning? Lungs on the verge of collapse? Good, that is when you know you need to push a little bit harder. It is at the brink of extreme physical exertion you find out who you truly are. Are you prepared to continuously suffer for another 5 hours because you have a goal, an ambition, a burning desire to complete something set out in front of you? 9 hours of physical activity wasn't my limit. The human will is limitless and physicality had nothing to do with it; it never really had in the first place. Endurance is an entirely psychological entity. I had more to give and I knew that when Percy and I were back safe and dry, I was going to become an IRONMAN. Barring King Kong coming back and stepping on my head, nothing was going to stop me completing the run. Running was my passion and I knew that if I had to crawl round on bloodied palms and grazed knees then I would have done.

Similar to the bike, the run was made up of laps, 8 lots of 3.2 miles this time. Perfect, I've got to run 8 5ks to become an IRONMAN. The support had now dwindled even more as we were hitting the early hours of Sunday morning and only the most hardy, committed supporters lined the running route, my partner included. You could tell they were also getting fatigued as their previously deafening clapping and whooping was gradually diminishing to solitary claps with a good 10-second pause between each one. I still mustered the energy to wave at those devoted supporters on each and every lap but couldn't help but notice even they had started to nod off after I had covered around 12 miles on the run. Lucozade didn't seem to be touching the sides any more as fatigue flooded my bones and with every step, energy seemed to seep out of my trainers into the tarmac.

The more committed triathlon wankers that were competing alongside me were rather frustratingly on their 8th running lap whilst I began my first. As they glided on past, their encouraging words were combined with also enthusiastically informing me what protein shake they were going to consume when they were finished (4 and a half hours before me).

'Stay in the moment, deal with the moment, Laura. It is no good focussing on the finish line at mile 12. Focus on getting to mile 13, then 14 and work out your next plan after that.'

There will forever be greater and lesser people than you in life, not just in triathlon. It would have been disastrously easy to allow the resentment towards 'triathlon Tim' to edge into my mindset. I could have allowed the green-eyed monster to convince me to belittle my own endeavour just because that bloke finished faster than me. If you finish a 10k in 35 minutes or 65 minutes, you still finished a 10k. If you finish a marathon in 6 hours or 3 hours, you still completed a marathon. Constantly comparing yourself and your achievements to others is not only hugely insecure and riddled with negativity, it also detracts away from your own success and progression. Take those insanely fast runners, overly efficient colleagues, skinny yummy mummies, friends who can do no revision and still ace their test, or whoever it is that you deem to be better than you, and use them as your fuel. Use 1-2% of your energy and acknowledge your perception that they are more successful than you (quash that ridiculous perception) then put the other 98% into celebrating every single one of your victories, no matter how trivial. Celebrate the fact you went out and ran 1 mile, even if you had planned to do 10. Do not focus your precious attention on the fact your mate from running club has done 15 miles today. They are not you; they are not on your journey, they have not faced your obstacles and despite what they have accomplished, it should never, ever devalue any of your personal achievements or success.

I congratulated my fellow competitor on their epic achievement, grabbed an unpleasantly warm energy gel from my short pocket and cracked the hell on. That would be me crossing that finishing line in a few hours and I was quietly excited about it already. I perversely quite like it when an event makes you run past the finish line 7 times on the running route (so agonisingly close you can literally touch it) before properly being allowed to cross it. That finishing arch arrogantly teased me, as I slogged it out and fantasised about finally getting to cross it. It's almost quite sadistic but at the same time, an invaluable tool for developing resilience and determination. I did not allow the thought of finishing to overwhelm me. I kept it in my brain as motivation only and didn't allow the constant reminder of the finishing arch on every lap to distract me from my well-established plan.

I'm not sure whether energy gels are supposed to be refrigerated or not. I do know attempting to swallow one after its been rattling about in your short pocket for 2 hours is like liquidising an out of date oyster, leaving it out in the mid-afternoon sun for 2 hours and letting it seep down your neck like a blind slug. Nevertheless, it was sugar, portable energy. I necked it and became ever closer to ending the relentless mocking from the finish line arch. My incredible partner had ventured out of the hotel room after about 3 and a half hours sleep and willed me on for the last few miles. Another fantastic support troop were blaring out 80's classics like they were seasoned Saturday night DJ's and, before I knew it, I was in the last mile of the marathon. This fiery ambition that had been burning literal and metaphorical holes in my pocket, social life, mental health and arse cheeks for months and months was finally in reach.

I struggled to hold back the tears forming in the corner of my eyes as I realised I could finally run through the finish line on this lap, not just past it. The lump in my throat was a minor inconvenience in actually trying to breathe for the last 200 metres but the feeling of elation at crossing under that line in 14 hours 35 minutes and 51 seconds was just unimaginable. The amalgamation of euphoria, fatigue, relief and unbridled pride was overwhelming and it could do nothing but manifest itself in uncontrollable crying. I'd done it. I'd bloody done it.

I WAS AN IRONWOMAN.

The beautiful orange and silver medal was placed around my wetsuit-chafed neck and I experienced that very unique and rare feeling of being 'enough'. For that finish line, that moment and for a good few days afterwards, who I was, what I was and what I had achieved was enough. I could revel in my triumph and actually relax momentarily as I sat in the rest and recovery phase of my life – which never seemed to last long. I was 'enough' in my mind for those couple of weeks because I had reached my goal. I was content, proud and happy. But, the goalposts are forever moving in life. Life isn't measured by how many medals are hanging on your personalised holder, but the ability to set a life-changing goal, achieve it, be incredibly proud of it and then go out and search for the next pursuit that is going to push your limits even further. Success to me is about continuous growth and relentlessly being the best version of yourself you can possibly be and if others can find inspiration in that – then it is a bonus. I'd sit and eat doughnuts marinated in ice cream for a few weeks, then go on the hunt for the next adventure that was going to extinguish the fire of ambition that was already starting to ignite yet again.

Chapter 5.

MARATHON 1 - Hang On We've Got a Problem Here...

"So, Laura, why choose to do 10 marathons in 10 days? Why not 8 or 9?"

"10-10-10, it just rolls off the tongue quite nicely, I suppose."

The local media attention my 10-10-10 challenge was attracting was growing daily and that always seemed to be the go-to question of every enthusiastic, but incredibly nasal radio presenter I was gladly interviewed by. Why do so many of them sound as though their entire nasal canal is blocked? I suffer very proudly with a face for radio, but surely there must be some sort of pre-requisite for a mildly tolerable tone of voice? You wouldn't quite expect the soothing tones of Joanna Lumley, but maybe something slightly gentler on the ears than a Barber Shop Quartet with a cold. However, I never had a complete answer to that question. I suppose it is like asking So Solid Crew why it was only '21 seconds to go' not '22.' Or asking David Beckham why he had to be number 7, not number 8. However, the more I thought about it, 2020 did represent 10 years since EAAA came to save my life and 10 marathons is far more impressive than 8 or 9. And there is always that one individual that gets funny about leaving the radio volume on an odd number, so a nice even 10 it was. I couldn't wangle much more time off work either... Anyway, it was March 2020 and the plans for my 10-10-10 challenge were in full swing. We were more than prepped and ready to start our 262 miles on Friday 17th April to finish on The Mall in front of Buckingham Palace for the tenth and final marathon on Sunday 26th in our brilliant Capital city.

I had been offered (and gladly accepted) a Gold Bond Place with the East Anglian Air Ambulance charity for the London Marathon on April 26th2020. Apparently, surviving a head-on battle with an articulated lorry and then having your life saved by this incredible charity gives you a VIP pass to run 26.2 miles around the streets of London for them. Well, it was an honour to be a representative of EAAA. All I had to do was raise £2,500 to secure my place. That's the real reason why 10-10-10 was actually born. Yes, my existence can essentially be broken down in to simply jumping from one extreme endurance challenge to the next and this just happened to be the next. Yes, I had to relieve the insatiable itch to continuously overachieve and do something extreme. Yes, I had to improve on my previous challenge of an IRONMAN. But, if I'm brutally honest, it just didn't sit right with me, to ask for £2,500 sponsorship to cover a solitary distance I had already conquered 6 times previously. So,

I thought, let's make it bigger. Let's do something that people will be proud to throw a fiver at.

So again, I gladly revisited the life philosophy of being the best version of yourself you can possibly be. For some, running 1 marathon in their lifetime is the pinnacle of achievement. For others, getting to 5k distance is their personal goal achieved. For the majority, maintaining their health, playing 5-a-side twice a week and cycling to work when the sun is out is their lot. Do you know what? Whichever category you fall into is absolutely fine. Some do no exercise whatsoever (I personally think they are missing out massively) but are happy with it. However, I had learned by now, as soon as you start to push the boundaries of these categories, you are inevitably met with doubt, a little bit of negativity and a question around whether what you're are doing is actually achievable. As soon as you start to promote or advertise an idea that is beyond the realms of personal potential for the masses, you'll start to receive doubt or negativity. This is often disguised as a well-intentioned comment or humorous remark.

"OH MY GOD, YOU ARE CRAZY?"

"THAT IS AN INSANE CHALLENGE. WILL YOU NOT GET INJURED?"

"THAT IS MENTAL. YOU'VE ALWAYS BEEN A BIT MAD THOUGH, BIRDY!"

People use it as a defence mechanism without even realising. As long as they label an extreme challenge that someone else is trying to achieve as mad or void of rational thinking, then it reassures them it is ok for them not to be doing it, or attempting it. In their mind, they have now categorised what I am attempting to do as unhealthy or irrational, therefore it is perfectly acceptable for them not to be doing it. And by verbalising that in an open forum such as social media or electronic communication, they have effectively backed themselves up and solidified their own limited thinking. Not so mad after all, is it?

Either I am wired slightly differently or I just think differently. I find it a little bit "mental" when others have the opportunity to absolutely grab life by the balls but choose not to. I find it crazy that instead of trying to better themselves in some small way, people lay stagnant in their comfort zones because it is warm and cosy in there. But you can guarantee those in their warm and cosy comfort zone will be the first to criticise anyone trying to break out of it because it then questions their life choices. If you are happy in your comfort zone and have no desire to experience a little bit of anxiety, stress or hardship for a longer-term achievement, then fine. But don't ever try to bring down someone else who is putting themselves out there and trying to do better, or trying to improve themselves in some way.

You don't have to run a marathon to do better or be better. You don't even have to run at all (I'm just a bit biased about that). It can be far simpler than that. Teaching yourself a language, attempting to make a new recipe in the kitchen, reading a book to educate yourself on a new topic you are interested in, getting off the bus two stops before home so you have to walk a bit further, washing those dishes up at 10:30pm just before bed so you don't have to do them in the morning. There are little challenges in every single day that I like to call opportunities. They are all opportunities to try and be a little bit better and push those boundaries of your own comfort zone, no matter how big or small you perceive it to be.

From the day 10-10-10 was born, I had absolutely no psychological doubt in my mind that I would complete it. I don't trust myself not to get injured. I don't trust myself not to get ill. I don't trust myself not to say something stupidly controversial and piss someone off when trying to achieve something. But I have complete and unreserved trust in my psychological resilience, in my ability to deal with discomfort, to continue through brutal conditions and to stubbornly and doggedly persevere with whatever situation is placed in front of me. In reality, long, arduous physical challenges have very little to do with physical fitness. It is 20% physical and 80% a pure, distinct, unrivalled desire to never give up. So, in December 2019, planning for 10-10-10 begun.

Emails began flying around to nutrition companies, physiotherapists, trainer companies, other endurance athletes, energy gel inventors, sports drinks brands, bath salt companies, running sock companies, clothing brands, more physiotherapists, sports bra fitters, sweatband knitters, specialist shoelace creators, bakers, T-shirt fakers and candlestick-makers. You would not believe the depths some of these ambitious companies will go to, just so you have a slightly more pleasurable running experience. I was absolutely lapping it up. This brilliantly positive focus gave some welcome, light relief from the relentlessly negative environment I was suffering as a Police Officer at the time. I couldn't wait to get home from a 9-hour slog immersed in death, violence, a worryingly broken system and authority walking round like their shit doesn't stink, to check if I'd been offered some free blister plasters for my challenge. So much of the time, I hadn't. But, when a company so much as donated a free bottle of water and an encouraging word to the cause, I grew in confidence. A little bit more support, a little bit more exposure. Imagine the bloody party I had when 30 free energy gels and bars came through the post from RawVelo, a vegan energy gel company (the very sort you bump in to at IRONMAN registrations). The hard graft planning was eventually paying off in the form of product donations, as well as plenty of pennies for the fundraising pot.

Training, as we have already probably established, came quite naturally. If I have a purpose, if I have a goal, if I have something I am personally accountable for – I'll train like an animal. It is like the end goal is my master and I am the submissive animal that will answer every command to appease my leader. I was so focussed on getting the mileage in, it was never a slog. It was just as though every single little mile I covered was chipping away at this big old goal I'd set. I'd start at 10 miles on a Monday, 11 miles on the Tuesday and add a mile every day until I did 16 miles on the Saturday. I'd grind out hill sprints after 5-mile tempo runs. I'd get up at 6am and run 5 miles and then do exactly the same at 6pm for 3 or 4 days on the bounce. I'd be hitting 80-90-mile weeks for a good 6 weeks in preparation. The whole project just became my world.

The next question was where. We had to find 10 suitable places to run a marathon. Places where we weren't going to become totally de-motivated by looking at the same field for 5 hours, but also places that meant something, places that were accessible for others to join in for a few miles, places we were going to remember, places that weren't going to take a 3-hour tussle with the M25 to get to. Every single runner has experienced that eagerly anticipated response to the statement,

"I'm running a marathon..."

"Oh, is that London?"

"No, it's actually taking place in Cambridge."

"Oh, lovely and how far is that then?"

It appears to be completely inconceivable to any individual that isn't so exposed to the running community, that there could possibly be another, scheduled, organised, competitive 26.2-mile foot race that isn't the London Marathon.

We decided that looped routes or out and back routes would be preferable to just running and running until the watch tipped 26.2. We needed to have a base that we could return to once every few miles if my toenails were hanging off or I needed to intravenously insert Haribo into my system. So, eventually, we had our list. We came up with 10 locations that meant something, weren't a million miles away and could be inclusive to people who wanted to come and join in.

There it was: Ipswich, Alton Water, Thetford Forest, Royston, Brighton, Hove, Grafham Water, St Ives, Cambridge, London. Our 10 locations set and ready to be run around. Routes were planned. Posters had gone out. Fundraising was flying. Bake-sales. Bring and Buy sales. Charity auctions for running equipment and books. The miles were in the bank. We were just 2 weeks away from starting marathon 1 when an unknown, unpredictable, quite terrifying creature started prowling around our territory, pissing all over our already marked lampposts. Not just my territory either – the whole fucking world's.

I'm quite sure I'm not the only one who still shudders when they hear the word Coronavirus. Initially, the unavoidable banter started and this was just a little sniffle you caught after drinking one too many of the well-known Mexican bottled beers. But before we knew it, this tragic, unexplained, unidentified, unchartered disease came along, pulled the whole world's pants down and gave it a huge slap on the arse. I'm also quite sure you didn't buy this book to read about Coronavirus; we are all experts by now anyway, aren't we? All you really need to know is that it scuppered our plans. It completely and entirely trashed all of our plans. As soon as London Marathon pulled the plug on their race (the first time they had ever had to do that since 1981), there was no point even trying to continue with my 10-day bender.

The world just turned into this whirlwind of negativity and my glorified endurance run paled into insignificance. People were dying in their thousands, losing their jobs and in some cases, losing their sanity. Thankfully I hadn't lost any of those things, not yet, but I had, temporarily, lost my purpose. Almost simultaneously, 3 of the marathon locations, Thetford Forest, Grafham Water and Alton Water, shut their doors to the public and showed no imminent sign of re-opening. The world was being told to stay indoors and very few now had a spare penny to throw in the fundraising pot. The huge shining beacon of light in all of this utter madness was that I could still run. The country could still run. We were still allowed out for a reasonable amount of time in a day for exercise, which to me, is a testament to just how important exercise is in itself. The country seemed to be crumbling at its knees but going out and putting one foot in front of the other was still high enough on the priority list to be allowed. Of course it would be; even in a global pandemic, a twenty-minute run will solve more problems than you thought imaginable. I almost felt proud of running. I felt proud that the pursuit that had accompanied me through so many of life's peaks and troughs was now the highlight of the day for thousands who didn't even acknowledge it existed beforehand.

So, we did what we were told. We sat and waited and bided our time and hoped that this would all go away as quickly as it came about. It didn't and hasn't but the country was still being illuminated every day with unbelievable acts of kindness and hard work from volunteers, strangers and our wonderful NHS. Although, I won't deny that I played the starring role in my own self-created shit show for a few days. I sulked, stomped around for a bit and felt sorry for myself because, having been wearing my positive pants for so long, they had been ceremoniously replaced with an ill-fitting G-string that was getting more irritating by the day.

In order to start working back up the hill, at the bottom of which my 10-10-10 challenge had found itself, I did the only thing I knew how to do at that point, which was to run. To celebrate what would have been the original start date of 10-10-10, I committed to doing a 'Lockdown Marathon.' It was incredibly convenient that my local park had a near-exact perimeter of 0.26 miles, meaning I would have to do 101 laps of it to equal a marathon. This is exactly what I did do and it was such a turning point. There was no big pasta party the night before, no nervous sleep in a busy city hotel, no panicking over whether I'd remembered to pack enough gels or trainers, no totally irrational thoughts about the organisers running out of medals or tripping up a kerb, no eating 23 bowls of porridge at breakfast to make sure you'd had enough and no forcing a poo out at 6am because you fear what you might catch from the start-line 'Portaloos.'

I got up when I wanted, had 1 bowl of porridge, walked the 2 minutes to the park with energy gels in my pocket and drink in hand and started to run. I was ticking off lap after lap and (albeit getting a bit dizzy) getting into a solid rhythm. I didn't have to speed up because there was a big crowd round the corner, I didn't have to slow down to grab the 1 and a half sips of water left in the cup being held out by the smiley volunteer. I didn't have asthmatic Alan breathing down my neck at mile 16, slowly covering my neck in his sweaty spittle. By 11:30am, my marathon was done and, from that day forward, it became a distance, nothing more, and nothing less. That big, scary word that intimidates people all over the world was a distance to cover and that was it. Slowly but surely, 10-10-10 started to live and breathe again and a small amount of momentum, both in the challenge and myself, was restored.

Of course, the days, weeks and months seem to drag when you are waiting for something to happen. You will always perceive time to be going slower when you are in an undesirable predicament. I was certainly in no position to complain. I'm sure the front-line emergency service staff (who had been in a mildly undesirable predicament 12 hours a day for 2 months) were all pretty keen for Coronavirus to do one as well. But that couldn't stop me being like an excitable kid on the countdown to Christmas, eagerly and intently watching every news bulletin to monitor the severity of what the country was going through to see if it was going to be safe enough to get the challenge back on the road. Gradually, the country started to ease its very limiting restrictions and as our Prime Minister's golden, wavy locks grew longer and longer, so did, very importantly, the amount of time we were allowed to spend outside.

"I think we should go for it, Mand."

My comment was quite spontaneous and caught my partner (my best friend, biggest supporter and would-be support bike) rather off guard. I tended to forget that other people had different thoughts infiltrating their headspace over a 24-hour period. Whereas my brain (what little room there is in there) had been entirely saturated with thoughts of the challenge for 6 months and any potential sniff of getting closer to actually doing it was only going to further fill the old grey matter.

"Go for what?" she replied, thinking I was referring to some sort of takeaway for dinner.

"The challenge!" I said abruptly, again carelessly forgetting there are actually different things happening in the world other than what is floating around my head.

"I'm ready. I'm so ready and according to the national news, so is the country."

It was as though I was an articulate teenager pleading with their parents to invest in a puppy, detailing all the joy, positivity and health benefits it would bring, but quickly breezing over the undeniable financial implications, lack of sleep, physical fatigue and massive life commitment it would also bring. In my mind, the new puppy was already pissing on the kitchen floor, Amanda didn't take much convincing and with that, the new date was set; Friday, June 12th 2020 we would be ready to go again.

The seemingly bottomless blue IKEA bags had been stacked full of Lucozades, energy gels, protein flapjacks, new socks, plasters and inner tubes for months now. There was literally no more organising to do. Because some Coronavirus travel restrictions were still lingering and there was still a lack of overnight accommodation open, we had to adapt the locations slightly. Our 10 locations were whittled down to Ipswich, Bar Hill, Holywell, Felixstowe, Cambridge, Brighton, The Guided Bus, Thetford Forest, Grafham Water and St Ives.

I was so pumped I thought my hyperactive feet were going to break through the footwell of our packed-out silver Kia and we were going to 'Fred Flintstone' it the whole way to Marathon 1. It was like a testing game of Tetris slotting everything in the car before we left. You certainly don't develop an appreciation of what it takes to be self-sufficient for endurance events before you actually take them on yourself. With every spare water bottle, energy bar, piece of recovery equipment, shoelace and t-shirt you can imagine, we finally arrived in Ipswich for day 1, Marathon 1.

I was just so appreciative and happy to actually get running, to get in my stride, to do what I do best after being on hold for so long. A little gathering of my sisters, old school friends and teachers had huddled (a safe distance from one another) outside the start point of the local Community Centre. It was so encouraging to see them all there. People from my home town were coming out to cycle, walk and run alongside me. Initially, it almost felt a bit anti-climactic, that we were just heading out on another run which, essentially, we were. In order to maintain the positive mindset I needed, I'd resigned myself to the idea we were just heading out on another run, day after day. I had to forget I was covering 262 miles over the course of 10 days, otherwise, I would begin to overthink and let that destructive negativity creep in. Stay in the moment, deal with the moment.

The anti-climactic feel of day 1 soon faded and I was ashamed I'd even experienced that emotion as I trotted around the old trails and cycle paths of where I grew up, remembering mass games of 'Manhunt' in the woods or 25-a-side games of football in the summer evenings of years gone by. Parents of old school friends who I hadn't spoken to in years had written motivational messages in huge writing on whiteboards and proudly placed them on their front lawn. Another old school friend had set up a table of Jelly Babies and water bottles and sat on her driveway, with her 12-week-old baby, patiently waiting for us to run past. There was absolutely no malice in why we hadn't spoken in years; life just happens and you inevitably drift apart. But the community I appeared to be bringing together on just day 1 was nothing short of inspiring. People wanted to be a part of this adventure; people were craving a small amount of positivity in a world that had been brought to its knees with adversity for months. The kindness and generosity that our human race is so capable of broke out and shone in all its charitable glory for the whole 26.2 miles. An old school teacher came whizzing past on his bike, (that I'm sure was just as rusty and rickety as it was the last time I saw it 12 years ago) and shouted encouragement from the road at mile 10. Another teacher's 7-year-old twin girls cycled the first 6 miles without a word of complaint and thanked ME for the opportunity!

We seemed to be flying for the first 18 miles, being joined mile after mile by supportive friends and well-wishers, more than happy to plod along for 5k to the beat of 'Eye of the Tiger'. The planned route was 4 laps of 10k so it was easy for fellow runners to jump in and out as they pleased. It is completely expected in a 'normal' marathon to hit the 20-mile blues and have to grind out the last 6 miles on pure willpower alone. But this was far from a 'normal' marathon – it was anything but. The terrible twenties didn't so much as touch my seemingly invincible legs and my support team and I strode along the Main Road of Kesgrave Town with such gusto it was as though we were smashing out 400 metres on a sunny sports day.

A jubilant gang of supporters cheered me across the finish line in exactly the same location we had left just 4 hours and 21 minutes earlier. I was completely euphoric. The last 6 months of my life had been dedicated to this undertaking and the first day couldn't have gone any better. My sister Ellie cycled the whole 26.2 miles on a bike that passed its sell-by date at least 10 years ago, my dad smashed out a half marathon, my closest friends came and finished the last 5 miles with me. We were starting to create a following and I bloody loved it. I'm not ashamed of the fact I love being the centre of attention, which for the most part, I was. But it was becoming everything I wanted it to be, encouraging others to run, walk, and cycle and to become immersed in this positivity bubble we were quickly establishing. Even if they didn't want to run, using some worn-out felt tip pens to make a sign with the kids and grabbing what was left of the Jelly Babies after I had devoured them, gave them reason to smile and feel included in what was going on. It was time to shove copious amounts of carbohydrates down my neck, whack the recovery compression boots on, flood social media with my rampant positivity and get ready for day 2.

Don't get me wrong, waking up on day 2, I knew I'd run a marathon the day before, but the feeling was different. Typically, upon completing 1 organised marathon, you feel euphoric, consume numerous alcoholic beverages, demolish a dirty burger and assume an ice bath is what your next bottle of champagne is being served in, not what you should be sitting in. The weight of your monumental task has been lifted from your shoulders and you can celebrate and relax with your lactic acid-infused legs, knowing full well if you walk like you've shat yourself for a week, it didn't matter, your job was done. On day 2, my job most certainly wasn't done; I'd barely even passed my probation. I knew that and as much as I'd have liked the completion of my first of 10 marathons to be followed by a boozy evening of takeaway curry and gently caressing my own ego, I knew I wouldn't make it past day 4 if I behaved like that. The challenge became more of a personal responsibility for me day by day; I was accountable for the success or failure of the 10 days. I woke up slightly sore, but my exhilarating evening the night before, brimming full of pasta, protein shakes and pressure point foam rolling, had got me more than ready for day 2.

Marathon 2 was set in Bar Hill, a friendly little village on the outskirts of Cambridge where I had lived previously for a number of years. Bar Hill was scattered with loyal friends who I knew I could depend on to give me a kick up the arse should I have required one over the 26.2-mile route. Bar Hill also had just a handful of (as the name would suggest) steep, graduating, energy-sapping hills and my plan to run around the 2.5-mile ring road 10.5 times would mean I would encounter approximately 22 hills throughout the route. That wasn't your best plan to date, was it, Laura? A local TV crew had the camera set up and were waiting for a pre-marathon interview in the social club car park. Not only did I feel like a very minor 'E-list celebrity, it was another opportunity to quietly enjoy the successful outcome of an email trail that started in February. Those doors certainly didn't open themselves; I'd been banging on every door I could for the previous 4 months so every little publicity boost really meant a lot. Interview done and with another cracking turn out of friends, family and well-wishers at the start line, we began lap 1 of 10.5 on day 2.

As expected, Bar Hill did not disappoint. Around every corner was another animated family offering ice pops, Lucozade, Jelly Babies, financial donations and freshly cut oranges on a blisteringly hot day in South Cambridgeshire. They all wanted to be a part of the campaign and I was so indebted to every single one of them. The support came in waves throughout the first 2 hours. It was perfectly timed so that whenever I'd periodically reach a low point, it wouldn't be long before there was another frantic supporter around the next corner to boost the moral once more. However, despite the copious amounts of ice pops devoured, clammy pats on the back and factor 50 sun cream slathered over every inch of my body, it was stiflingly hot. I always find extremes of weather conditions a fantastic opportunity to learn something about oneself. First and foremost, there is quite literally nothing I or anyone can do to control the weather; it will unashamedly do whatever it likes. I can, quite easily, mind you, control my reaction to it, as can anybody for that matter. Complaining about the heat or the cold will not benefit me in any way. It will only add fuel to that slight spark of negativity in the back of my mind, that will rage into a full-blown fire if allowed to. You have to apply every necessary adaptation to deal with an extreme of temperature (abundance of fluids, sun hat, frequent dousing in cold water, sun cream, seeking out any form of shade, the odd mini strop to vent a bit of frustration, a couple of ice pops) and crack on with it. Or at least that is exactly what we had to do to deal with the tropical temperatures of day 2.

We'd experienced a mini heatwave in the days building up to 10-10-10 and I'd already received the unpreventable barrage of (unconscious, unintentional) social media negativity,

"I bet you're glad you are not running in this!!"

"Thank Goodness the challenge wasn't this week!"

"Oh, you'd die if you had to run a marathon in this!"

It takes a lot more for me to die than a bit of heat, believe you me! If I would have had to run in 30-degree heat as per the conditions in the week before the challenge, then I would have done. We would have carried on regardless and ignored the individuals who appear to be entirely governed by external elements. I never forget overhearing one elderly woman during one of the pre-challenge shopping trips that happened to be taking place on one of the aforementioned heatwave days. Whilst I was piling up more beige carbohydrates and sugary snacks into my trolley, I heard her proudly exclaim to the entirety of the cheese counter staff,

"OH, IT IS ABSOLUTELY UNBEARABLE OUT THERE!!"

Unbearable? Unbearable?! I think you are pronouncing 'hot' incorrectly, my love. Personally, I would use the word unbearable to describe prolonged physical torture, the sudden, unexplained death of a young child or being exposed to any form of deep, drawn-out physical or psychological suffering. The use of the word 'unbearable' encourages connotations of warfare, terrorism, rampant morbidity or unbelievable human tragedy, not getting a bloody sweat on in the deli counter queue at the back of Morrison's. Jesus. Choose your words wisely. That woman, completely of her own merit, has transformed her mindset to associate a beautiful warm day with something totally atrocious. Instead of finding a bit of shade, downing an ice-cold pint of anything wet (and by the state she was in, hopefully alcoholic,) and being appreciative of a bit of sunshine, she has determined her temperament for the rest of the day with one negative, lonely statement. I always take careful consideration of the language I am using to describe a situation to ensure it isn't unnecessarily dramatic...

Anyway, I continued in the unbearable heat around Bar Hill and attacked every incline with as much spirit as I could muster, safe in the knowledge that every uphill had a downhill to look forward to as well. My high expectations of the Bar Hill support crew were surpassed and I didn't run 1 mile of the marathon alone. Every 2.5-mile lap I was accompanied by energetic cyclists and runners, who themselves were all dealing with the temperatures and undulating route as well.

The fresh pot of Vaseline, which was only purchased as a standby medical supply, had very quickly become my best friend and we were becoming rather intimate with each other, even on day 2. I thought we might dip into it in the latter stages of the week when the inevitable skin chafing was sticking to my sweat-drenched clothes, but evidently, I would require it a lot sooner than that. The heat, combined with my sweat, with an added dash of spilt Lucozade as well as my clothes' unrivalled desire to stick to me, caused my sports bra to lovingly chafe across the first few layers of the skin and remove most of it just under my well-supported boobs. By a couple of hours into day 2, my special Star Wars plaster had rubbed off and my upper body undergarment was already drawing blood from the repetitively irritated wound. I was sadly misled by the deceitful packaging, reassuring me that Chewbacca, R2-D2 or Luke Skywalker would protect and repair any wound they were faced with. They may have been able to save a galaxy far, far away but they did not protect my red raw skin from being chafed by my sports bra. That was by no means my biggest worry and I think, by that point, my pain threshold could hold out without the need for overpriced film-themed plasters, but my Christ, it was sore. Relentlessly and repetitively sore. The air and dry environment those layers of skin needed to heal was not going to be very readily available over the 8-day period left to run; that wound was going to be wet and sweaty for at least 6 hours a day for the remaining 8 days on the bounce. Amanda attentively slathered the wound in Vaseline at our 2.5-mile checkpoint on the Bar Hill route in the hope the sticky, mucus gunk would provide a much-needed layer of protection from the overly clingy bra. The Vaseline did its job to the best of its ability but the sports bra scar (as it became affectionately known) was a perpetual reminder that maybe, even the most specifically designed sports apparel wasn't designed for this sort of demand. The only option I was left with was to run the next 8 marathons completely topless. There were a number of reasons why I chose not to continue with this option:

1. I was in enough discomfort as it was – I didn't need 2 black eyes to add to the injury list.

2. I didn't need all the offers from local modelling and Bay Watch impersonation companies flooding in – I just didn't have the time for my inevitable modelling career to take off so prematurely.

3. Getting arrested for outraging public decency would have certainly got more publicity for the challenge, but would have probably impacted slightly on the tight schedule.

4. I had enough brilliant company and support as it was – I didn't need local naturist groups joining in on the fun as well.

5. My good friend Emily had designed and bought the most fantastic T-Shirts for the challenge listing all the consecutive dates and locations. Quite frankly, I needed those T-Shirts to know exactly where we were, where we were going next and what day it was. I wasn't letting them go to waste.

The pot came out once again in quite an unexpected fashion not long after sports bra scar-gate. The unenviable mixture of salty sweat and droplets of sun cream began streaming into my eyes as the heat became more intense. So, the Vaseline pot was delved in to once more to, this time, provide a viscous barrier across my two eyebrows to prevent the pesky sun cream/sweat combo creeping into my eyes. Typically, most would rely on the protective capacity of their eyelashes to do this for them, but the volume of sweat/sun cream dripping from my forehead and my noticeable shortage of eyelashes required the Vaseline wall for support. This shortage of eyelashes had never proved a problem before. But I had never needed them as much as I did on Marathon day 2.

'Why an earth did you have a shortage of eyelashes?'

I can almost hear you asking the question under your breath. The very simple answer to that question is because I pull them out. If I'm unnecessarily fretting about overdoing it a bit or putting myself under a bit of pressure for a period of time, I bizarrely find a bit of relief in pulling out eyelashes. This very often leads to rather embarrassing and noticeable gaps. I've done it for as long as I can remember and found it incredibly strange until only a few years ago when I discovered it was 'a thing.' The compulsion to pull one's hair, often exaggerated by stress or anxiety, is known as Trichotillomania. Trust me, look it up; that tongue twister of 'T's and 'L's is a medically recognised condition. As with all psychological and physical diagnoses, there are varying scales of it. I believe mine to be relatively minor -

I get a bit 'edgy' about something and I unconsciously start tugging at my eyelashes; almost like biting one's nails. Others suffer to the extent where they pull clumps of hair from their scalp and can even put themselves in grave danger by eating what they pull out. The hair can coagulate in their stomach and, if repetitively done for long enough, even lead to death. I've been known to regularly have 3 breakfasts, a mid-morning snack and a light lunch before 11am on a long run day, but even I'm not at the stage of wanting to do that. The scale of Trichotillomania to that extent must be really awful to comprehend and deal with. However, I don't make a fuss or use its posh name as the reason my rare application of mascara looks a bit skew whiff. I pulled them out, that's my doing and my responsibility and I'll carry on working at it so that removing my eyelashes isn't my go-to when I'm overthinking things a bit. I'm not going to pull out of marathon number 2 because my eyelashes aren't as protective as they could be and the membranes covering my eyeballs were stinging like they've been intimate with a scotch bonnet for a few hours. I'll just accept it is my problem, whack a wall of Vaseline on my eyebrows and get on with it.

I get immeasurably frustrated at our current society having to label things or name things in order to justify unsuitable, rude, strange or illegal behaviour. It constantly feels like an excuse to me when people of all walks of life(not just young people) who have no social boundaries, no social understanding or are just plain rude manage to escape punishment or reprimand because their poor behaviour is due to an acronym they have been given that governs their life. I'm sure the diagnoses, when they do come, act as great relief to the majority of friends and family who have been struggling to ascertain why their loved one is so adamantly disobeying rules or behaving differently to others. I'm sure that living and coping with genuine cases of behavioural problems in people of any age is a tiring, debilitating and hard-fought battle with very limited rest and reward. I metaphorically take my hat off and bow to those dedicated, underappreciated, committed, hard-working individuals who devote their life to the care and development of their loved one. All I'm saying is call a spade a spade. If your loved one is being a shit for the sake of being a shit and they do know the boundaries between right and wrong but are curiously testing them, recognise that. If they are refusing to do something due to laziness but using their 'condition' as the excuse, have a bloody word. Don't shirk responsibility and blame directly disobedient behaviour on a diagnosis, which has plenty of other symptoms that don't include any of the ones being displayed in the most recent outburst.

After removing most of the eyelashes in my left eye and having a tantrum, I called day 2 off and blamed it on my Trichotillomania... Yeah right, I'd have sooner died than give up on my 10-day pursuit. 16 ice pops, 23 bottles of water and 7 separate applications of sun cream later and we were into the final 1.2 miles of day 2. As much as I believed my planning was entirely exact, that all the routes would tick over to 26.2 miles the second I crossed the planned finish line, it quite often didn't work like that. That dreaded moment every runner has experienced, when you peer down at your Garmin expecting it to read at least 26.1 and it is still on bloody 25.6 happened numerous times throughout the 10 days. And that last half a mile always seems to take 45 minutes. We were running up and down every nearby cul-de-sac, car park and corridor to clock up those precious last few metres before finally seeing the 26.2 ping up on the watch screen. We were greeted at the Bar Hill finish line with confetti cannons and celebratory cheers. Probably the hottest marathon I'd ever run was well and truly ticked off the list, and with 52.4 miles run in 2 days, there were just another 8 days to go to get through the remaining 209.6...

By days 3 and 4, I was becoming very good at distinguishing between discomfort and pain and learning that there is a considerable difference between them. Day 3 was a route around the sleepy, picturesque village of Holywell. Any individual running a marathon through their charming little suburb was potentially the most exciting thing to happen in Holywell since 2004. Not to mention the absolute pandemonium caused in the village by the East Anglian Air Ambulance crew strutting into the party for a mile or so around the halfway point. I panicked as I saw the bright yellow, EAAA emblazoned vehicle pull up around the corner, thinking someone had been genuinely hurt or there was some sort of emergency. It took a few seconds to engage my sleep-deprived brain and then be overjoyed that they had, of course, turned up to support me. What a relief and what an idiot. This was turning into the Holywell equivalent of an organised rave. The whole village can be circumnavigated on foot and the distance totalled just under a mile, so with the initial 3 miles completed with my run from home to Holywell, we needed to complete approximately 24 loops of the route to complete the third marathon. The homes that were dotted around the village were elegant yet humble and the residents retiring, but outwardly friendly. I'm sure, however, there was more than one 'curtain-twitcher' at the window when I was on lap 17 – the poor locals must have thought I was lost or just some sort of nonsensical rambler best left to their own devices. Which actually wasn't too far from the truth.

Surviving on a diet of energy drinks, flapjacks and jelly sweets for the past 72 hours was beginning to take its toll as I experienced the first real bout of 'discomfort' at around mile 18 on day 3. My body had been relentlessly questioning what an earth I was doing to it from day 1, but it nobly continued, just subtly making me aware of its disgruntlement with a strong feeling of nausea coupled with an emptiness that didn't seem to be combated any more with just sugar – my usual go-to during hunger pangs. By around 4 hours in, I sat down in the middle of the road, midday sun glaring down on my head and just began furiously retching. My stomach was trying to get rid of whatever had upset it, but there were very little contents in there to regurgitate. The involuntary stomach contractions were an unwelcome core workout to add to the other 26.2-mile warm-up that day. I very hesitantly started to fight the emptiness with a couple of salt and vinegar crisps that actually crunched down quite nicely. They very quickly became a staple mid-run snack. But this whole rather undignified incident was not painful; it was uncomfortable but it was tolerable. Yes, I wouldn't want to sprawl myself across Holywell ring road every weekend and hurl my guts up, but it wasn't insufferable, just mildly vexatious. This was a really important realisation. I can deal with discomfort; I can temporarily displace it somewhere else in my brain and focus on something more positive and less debilitating to get the job done. Discomfort is not pain, far from it, and I think we so often get the 2 confused to the extent that it limits us. There were only around 8 laps left to get through after my short break and I ticked those off 1 by 1 to get to the finish. We allowed lovely, sleepy Holywell to recover and get back to some sort of normality as we completed marathon 3, with another memorable finish line in just over 5 hours and 11 minutes. My loyal friends, Emily, Mr and Mrs Nay, Lottie, Jody, Jax, Sim and Sam had been gallantly helping me hobble round, lap after lap and patiently waited the majority of those 5 hours just to make sure I had some friendly faces to see me through to the bitter end. 'Friend' is described in the dictionary as,

'A person with whom one has a bond of mutual affection, typically one exclusive of family relations.'

Well, the bonds between those people and I were not just mutual, they were certified as unbreakable on day 3, just as they were every single day preceding and proceeding that Sunday. And we certainly didn't feel exclusive of a family relation; we were our own little family where the welcoming love, support, dedication and humour was rife within us all.

If we were headed to Felixstowe on day 4 for a family day at the beach, building sandcastles, guarding our chips from greedy seagulls and refreshing ourselves in the sea the moment a bead of sweat dripped from our brow, conditions would have been perfect. But we had another sweltering, sandy 26.2 miles to get through. The discomfort diary was already fully booked on the hour's journey to the seaside. My blueberry porridge was sitting pretty heavy and the trusty legs were starting to feel the 78.6 miles they had run in the past three days. Obviously, I tipped out of the car to greet the other expectant runners lining the seaside pier with a huge grin and some sort of terrible joke about dodgy porridge. Inside, I was feeling rather less buoyant. However, that to me was partly the beauty of what I was creating. Followers of this challenge now expected me to beam positivity regardless of what I was feeling or experiencing. I'd set a precedent. I had been such an advocate for finding positivity in even the most ominous situation; I had a responsibility to practise what I preached. The responsibility also became greater when there was a following of people showering me with daily support and good wishes. How dare I show up to my own event, my own idea, my own marathon with a face like a slapped arse just because I didn't feel well? I needed to own this challenge and portray the courage and fortitude that were the foundations of it in the first place.

I was so grateful of the old friends and school teachers who had made such an effort to be at my fourth start line. We were undoubtedly reaching people and inspiring them to get going and grind out a few miles themselves. That was enough inspiration for me in itself. To know that what we were trying to achieve was inadvertently encouraging others to better themselves too was a fantastic feeling. I said from the start that if what I was attempting to do benefitted just 1 person in some small way, then every 1 of the 262 miles would be worth it. After a good basting in factor 50, we were off along the promenade with a gorgeous view of the beach and the North Sea to hopefully keep morale high all day. At that time in the morning, it was so calm and tranquil. It was almost an impossible notion that in just a couple of hours' time, hundreds of sun worshippers and beach dwellers would descend on Felixstowe seafront in their masses.

Being blunt about day 4, I was not well. I tried to contribute to the chirpy conversation my fellow runners were having, but instead, I needed to concentrate on keeping the contents of my stomach exactly where they belonged. Trying to consume something solid, anything at all just to give me some calories was becoming an ever more testing task. I couldn't stomach anything. A delightful little ice cream company opposite Felixstowe pier were informed of the small task we were undertaking and were very forthcoming in providing me with a free

Snickers-flavoured ('marathon' to all those over 30) tub of ice cream. What a jolly appropriate and well-thought-out flavour choice. Or they could have been being facetious, I'm still not sure. Cold, easy to digest and no chewing involved, I thought this would be the perfect halfway treat to ease my unsettled stomach. In fact, it was exactly what I needed to consume to encourage what had been impending all morning. Within seconds of polishing off a child-size portion of ice cream, I was being violently sick all over Felixstowe Pier. I had wondered why the fish and chip shack parallel to my sick spot had been directing evil glares our way for the rest of the day. I can definitely confirm the ice cream did not taste as good second time around. But finally, after a good old tactical vomit, the nausea that had been troubling me all day had disappeared and after 15.8 really arduous miles, the final 10.4 didn't seem as daunting. With a quick apologetic wave to the fish and chip man and at least 3 bites of a flapjack to fuel the next few miles, we were off again and the marathon 4 finish line was getting ever closer.

Complete strangers were donating their hard-earned money to the pot as my sister Daisy diligently sat at the fundraising point all day long. I'm quite sure 50% of people thought she was some sort of information point, as she was asked where the toilets were at least 10 times. But when you also have young children who couldn't have been more than about 7, wilfully donating their birthday money because their Mum didn't have any cash, you know you have to keep plodding on regardless of how dreadful you feel. Skipping (or rather shuffling) past the donation point every 3 miles was a good grounding tool. It was a consistent reminder of what we were doing and why we were doing it. Yes, we were attempting to be a beacon of positivity in an environment of adversity and we were trying to be a stalwart advocate for mental health. But we were also fundraising for a life-saving charity. So, in addition to running, recovering, travelling, fuelling, hydrating, updating, promoting, unpacking, repacking, informing and still remembering to breathe, we had to remember to push the fundraising as well. We made £109 from the charitable people of Felixstowe and through the heat, turbulent tummy and sandy blisters, which the seafront also generously donated, we hit 26.2 miles. Almost immediately after crossing the finish line, I jumped into the North Sea. The surprisingly cold crashing waves were such a welcome contrast to my furnace-like legs that had covered 104.8 miles in 4 days. As we reminisced about another memorable day in the salty waves, I gained more confidence from knowing we were nearly halfway.

Even before getting home on day 4, I'd decided that Felixstowe was the peak; it wasn't going to get any worse than that. The illness, the conditions and the heat had hit their pinnacle; surely, we would not have a day that was any worse than that. Even with all its flaws, it was still an incredible day. Day 4 was a solid lesson in not only psychological resilience but yet again the sheer, gritty determination of the human body. Usually, after chucking your guts up, you set yourself up on the sofa for the rest of the day, with copious amounts of tea and dry bread and wait to feel slightly better. I'd told myself after regurgitating 12 hours' worth of food and liquid that I would damn well carry on and finish the marathon I was responsible for. If you change your mindset and what you want out of the day, being poorly may not actually be as limiting as you initially thought. If I can run a marathon feeling as rank as I did that day, I fear my level of severity to justify a sick day from work may have significantly increased.

"You are not coming to work because you have a cold, Laura? I'm pretty sure a few months ago you ran 26.2 miles after regurgitating most of your breakfast and an ice cream?"

I may have to work on my sick day stories from here on in.

I woke up on day 5 with the usual throbbing in my back and legs that were both kindly reminding me daily what I was putting my body through. On the advice of my very good friend Dr Jo (she is accustomed to looking after people in all sorts of bother at well-established international endurance events), I'd put a pin in boiling water and used it to impressively burst Barry and Brian the blisters. Crikey. The fluid that came out of those bad boys could have watered the Eden Project for 2 days. But as Dr Jo promised, they felt so much better afterwards and the philosophy of short-term pain for long-term gain exemplified itself once more. Day 5 was a meandering 26.2-mile route in and around Cambridge and the affluent villages that surround it. I was honoured to be joined on day 5 by Dr Scott Castel, a serving doctor with the East Anglian Air Ambulance. I didn't find out until about mile 17 on the day that it was his first-ever marathon. He had diligently kept quiet as he didn't want to detract the attention away from my achievements. I was completely over the moon when I found out. People were running marathons because I was facilitating it for them. Granted, we didn't have manned water stations every 4 miles handing out sophisticated energy drinks and I wasn't going to put a lovely thick shiny medal around their neck when they had finished. But I'd created such a warm and welcoming platform where people knew exactly what I was trying to achieve and where I was trying to achieve it. It meant literally anyone could come along and complete one of the greatest endurance achievements of their life, because we'd created a supportive environment for them to do it. Dr Scott would not have run a marathon that day were it not for the challenge and after sharing 26.2 miles with someone, irrelevant of how long you have known them for, you very promptly become firm friends. I was so proud of the following we'd created after just 5 days of running and I could almost guarantee from that point forward I wouldn't be running one step alone. Complete strangers were coming to join in and, not only support me, but also escape any of their own personal struggles through soaking up some of the positivity we were creating. We'd almost created a weird sort of osmosis. Every single location we took the challenge to, we completely saturated it with humour, energy, stamina and joy. Then, when anyone came along to be immersed in that environment, even just for a couple of miles, all of that positivity just diffused from the huge amount we had, into the people that joined in and needed a boost. It diffused from us into them and every person left our little bubble having been permeated with encouragement and joy and it was just so inspiring.

It was another beautiful day and the support was in full flow at the start line again for marathon 5. We set off as a solid group of 6 for the first couple of miles around Bar Hill and through Dry Drayton before we were left as a trio of Dr Scott, my dear friend Belinda and I heading into the beautiful surroundings of Cambridge. That brilliant woman cycled every single mile of 2 of the most demanding marathons that week and the beautiful smile did not leave her face the entire time. The hills were demanding through Madingley and into Cambridge but the arrival of another on-duty East Anglian Air Ambulance crew undoubtedly boosted the mood. The guys joined us for a mile or so, buoyantly cheering us up the hills which was another huge contribution to the positivity party we were having. More runners joined us at the halfway mark of day 5 as we entered the village of Girton. The distraction of interacting with people and hearing their hilarious running stories and very intimate life events was so humbling. I could have written a book with just the stories we were discussing over the 10-day period, from defecating in bushes mid-run, getting so lost even contemplating asking a cow for directions wasn't out of the question and gaining financial shares in baby food as those little fruit sachets became a staple of everyone's diet after I had finished running with them! Hitting 13.1 miles meant we had covered 118 miles in just over 4 days and we were going great guns to get day 5 completed and hit the halfway mark. After completing a beautiful loop of Girton and Histon, we were heading back through Cambridge, past the very tranquil American Cemetery and picturesque Madingley to head to the finish line in Bar Hill. Dr Scott, Belinda and I were so grateful for my good friend Karen coming to meet us as we plodded through the last 2 miles. That is just the sort of thing people were doing. Coming completely out of their way in really hot conditions to come and see us, make sure we were ok, throw Jelly Babies at our head, chuck water over us and shove a rocket up our arse. Her smiley face and warm words of encouragement were enough to get us to the 5th finish line in Bar Hill where we were met, yet again, by a gallant group of supporters cheering us home. My friendships were incredible before we had started this adventure, but I truly, truly learned what love and friendship were when I was so well supported every single time I was falling out of my own arse after 26.2 miles. It was relentless every single day for the first half of this monumental feat and I was so deeply moved by it all.

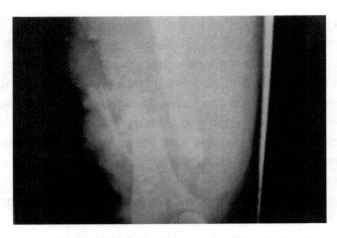

Anyone got any sticky tape? Apparently, the femur is the strongest bone in the body, but I did a very good job of making sure it was broken into two pieces

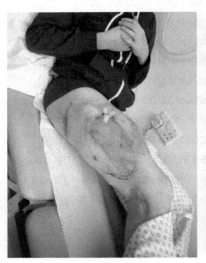

Almost two years after hospital admission, the reconstruction of my leg continued.

My 'Ray' of sunshine. Probably making a joke about me dropping it or tripping over.

Recruit #5 SAS: WHO DARES WINS 2019, SERIES 4

A true honour to run 26.2 miles with Dr Scott Castell. Yes, my socks look like a highlighter has leaked in them, I know.

Head down. Chest out. Chin up. One foot in front of the other. Applicable to life, not just running.

No finisher's medal will ever be able to live up to these 10 beauties.

At last, a decent-sized bottle that didn't contain water, Lucozade or some ghastly protein shake.

"Babe? Please can we have a takeaway tonight?" I don't think we'd ever held each other so tight.

The 10-10-10 community. The support I received was just phenomenal.

Chapter 6.
The Road to the A14

I'd always had a feeling I was a bit unique, a little bit against the norm, somewhat different to other little girls. I'm trying (and probably failing) to find a politically correct way of saying I flew in the face of just about every single stereotypical attribute you would associate with the female gender. I was that child on the exciting Friday afternoons in nursery, where everyone was encouraged to bring in their own toys, who brought in her mountain ranger Action Man figure. My beloved Action Man was equipped with his own off-road skateboard, red and black combat trousers, detachable hiking boots and an actual missile-firing, hand-held machine gun (can you tell I loved that toy a little too much?). Whilst Action Man and I were rescuing mountain goats from the top of the imaginary book corner mountain, every other female in the class was galloping with a 'My Little Pony' or plaiting the hair of one of those demonic plastic hairdressing heads. Surely, I had the right idea avoiding those things? They wouldn't have looked out of place in the prop cabinet of an elaborate horror film, where the bloody things take over the world, strangling defenceless children with their unbreakable plaited hair (can you also tell I had a few nightmares about those disgusting decapitated heads?). I still can't plait hair to this day and you'll still not find me within a mile of one of those things. Of course, one of the greatest elements of childhood is that precious innocence, which allows you to be exactly who you want to be for a few years, before societal expectations and conformity sets in. If I wanted to fight with the boys, play football, race my numerous Action Men across library books, eat mud and wear the same clothes (and underwear) 4 days in a row at 5 years old, there was apparently no problem. Add a few years on to that and all those rather boisterous, male-associated behaviours attract negative attention. Suddenly, who you actually are, and who society wants and expects you to be, become two very different things.

I'm still quite shocked to this day that I didn't come out of the womb with an eyebrow piercing, spiky hair and a tribal tattoo down my left forearm. There is literally not a time in my life that I can recall when I took some sort of pleasure or gratification from anything remotely feminine. I think I actively avoided anything that may be construed as 'girly' and was personally offended if any aspect of my life represented that of a little girl. I played every physical sport there was to offer and categorically refused to classify netball or dance as a sport. I even started a rather futile petition at school when the female students were forced into participating in netball and dance in year 9 whilst the boys got the joys of football and rugby. My petition categorically failed. But all I could derive from the sport of netball, being the stubborn, opinionated facetious little madam that I was, was that you had to stand still for 70% of the match and not move your feet, so that is exactly what I did. Stood still, sulked and didn't move my feet because I was being forced into a female-dominated pursuit which I had absolutely no interest in. Not much has changed from those school memories apart from this; I have since developed the utmost respect for netball, mostly because of wilfully watching the 2018 Commonwealth Games, where the England Women took home a glorious gold medal after one of the most intense 30 minutes of sport I had ever witnessed. If you have a spare hour, even if you have never watched a game of netball in your life, watch it. Anyone with even a slight affinity for sport, in general, will not regret it. That netball final represented every beautiful thing about sport in the most spectacular fashion. Netball, I apologise and I take back every derogatory gender-based insult I ever hurled at you.

My childhood wardrobe reflected the complete lack of interest I had in fashion or clothes, it was a sea of navy and grey, the only glimmer of colour shining from one of many adored football strips. I spent every spare moment kicking a ball with a group of lads, cycling across dirt tracks or watching repeats of 'Italia 90' on the television. I hated the thought of shopping, makeup, flowers, ear-piercing, Claire's Accessories, fashion, pamper parties, nail painting, general hygiene and anything and everything that would, even in the slightest of detail, remind me I was a girl. And, I was perfectly happy conducting myself in this manner. I adorned the same bowl haircut and un-pampered face for years until the cruel force of adolescence abruptly knocked me off my blissfully ignorant path and the less supportive section of my peers began to question my sexuality.

It wasn't only the superficial and material aspects of being a young woman I didn't want; I really struggled to come to terms with the physical changes too. I certainly didn't suffer to the extent of wanting to delve into the world of gender reassignment and decide to live the rest of my life as Lawrence. But every single natural, physical adaptation was a personal assault on who I wanted to be and what I wanted to achieve. I didn't want to have breasts; they would only hinder my ability to run and make it far more demanding to improve my time. Even more dramatically, it would mean I'd have to go into a 'ladylike' shop and actually purchase a sports bra. Use my hard-earned money to buy underwear that supports additions to my body I don't even want?! Or, the absolute killer blow, have a far too familiar female staff member measure my unwanted chest lumps? No. Periods? They can take a fucking running jump too. I didn't want to be a mother, I didn't have any maternal instincts and as for giving me extra bloody body fat to facilitate something I unquestionably didn't want, what is this?! A step by step guide on how to uncontrollably ruin your life?! I'll take the addition of extra body fat to facilitate my overzealous appetite for dodgy protein shakes, but for the ability to have periods – no thanks. It was that control factor again. These things were happening almost overnight and I had absolutely no control over them. Maintaining my famously stubborn streak, I just dug my heels in and headed as far in the opposite direction of effeminateness as I could. Every dreaded monthly arrival of the painters and decorators encouraged another purchase of an oversized football shirt or an even shorter haircut. I'm sure the only reason my poor teachers gave in and started a women's rugby club was just to shut me up (or to prevent another petition.)

My entire character, appearance and every single one of my mannerisms must have screamed lesbian with the customary illuminated neon arrow from about 6 years old and I couldn't have been much older than that when I knew myself. I was as straight as a roundabout and yet again, there was nothing I could do about it. I hardly did a decent job of hiding it or putting people off the scent slightly, but I would adamantly deny it at every possible opportunity. I was, quite conversely, so ashamed of it, ashamed that it was a part of me. I was bold as brass when it came to displaying all of these unruly, audacious traits and donning all of the least effeminate attire I could muster, but so disgusted by what it actually represented. My tomboyish nature made me exactly who I was and it was the only way I knew how to be, but as adolescence continued to take a hold, I grew to despise it even more. I did not want to be gay. I didn't have a choice as so many Neanderthals still believe. As I slowly but steadily continued to despise who I was, I decided to overhaul my behaviour and head back towards my dying female tendencies in a useless attempt to cover up who I was.

I started going out in the most ridiculous dresses you could imagine. I'm pretty sure one of the scraps of material I owned was actually a top (I'd still probably make the same mistake today.) I looked like a vacuum-packed leg of lamb some nights. I was being daringly promiscuous, insensibly promiscuous. All teenagers go through the phase of having a different boyfriend/girlfriend for every night of the week, like the novelty socks you get at Christmas, a pair for Monday, a pair for Tuesday etc. But I wasn't behaving this recklessly because I wanted to, I was doing it to prove a completely useless point. If I associate myself with as many boys as possible and wear skin-tight crop tops on a Friday night, that will surely outweigh and put into disrepute the other 6 days a week I spent in baggy tracksuits, 7days I spent on a football pitch and every other day of the week I paraded around like the 'laddish' hooligan I was in my late adolescence. There was nothing in the world that could 'put into disrepute' my lesbianism. I was gayer than a life-size PINK cut out, wearing a rainbow-collared shirt, sleeves rolled up to look more manly, with a Staffordshire bull terrier sat next to it, holding a pint of Fosters, watching 'The L-Word.' But I was still convinced I could persuade people otherwise because I couldn't bear the world knowing I was gay. The confusing circus in my brain completely accepted every other gay individual I knew (very few at the time) and celebrated them. But I was ashamed to associate the label with myself. Ultimately, the relentless battle between who I actually was and who I was trying to be was too much to contend with and contributed a huge step towards the decision made on the A14. I would have rather have been dead than admit to being gay.

My father leaving the family home had significant influence over my personality and who I became. It not only had an impact on my sexuality, but my entire upbringing and resulting behaviours. In fact, it was a combination of, at the time, both of my strikingly incompetent parents. I was solidly boyish even at the age of 7 when he left us and started a new life with another wife and new children. But his departure unconsciously encouraged a family promotion in my eyes. I now needed to become the man of the house. My mother was many things but one of her fundamental flaws as not only an adult but also a parent, was her near-complete dependency on others, including her children. Even at such a tender age, I knew I had to adopt adult characteristics in order for the house dynamics not to be too disrupted. I had to be a reassuring word every time ANY letter came through the post, just in case it was a letter from the solicitor, which always induced an evening of blind panic and anger. I had to be the face of stubbornness when any welfare officer disputed a 7-year-old's decision not to see her father and obstinately remain loyal to her oblivious mother. I had to be the brave voice at the end of a 999 call after my epileptic mother had another stress-induced seizure. I tiptoed on eggshells and never complained about a single thing just to ensure the house maintained a relatively happy atmosphere and even if there wasn't a good environment, I ensured I couldn't be directly to blame. I had to put my requests for *anything* on the back burner, just in case needing a glass of water might be what tipped things over the edge that day. This excessively fearful environment bred such a streak of self-doubt and anxiety in me and I wasn't even aware of it. Years and years of reluctantly coming home and never quite knowing whether blinking the wrong way upon arrival might set an increasingly adverse tone for the rest of the evening. Or constantly worrying that the foul mood your parent was in was directly because of you or something you had done, because the repercussions of it certainly weren't being felt by anyone else. I was forever undertaking chores around the home, off my own back, to make it spotless to reduce the chances of a messy house being the reason for the misery hanging over the home that day. My father leaving the family home was neither the fault of my brother or I but, at the time, it appeared we were the only ones suffering the consequences of the blame.

I was totally unaware of it at the time, but at the very tender and impressionable age of around 8, I was stuck in a constant cycle of avoiding punishment, outwardly doing unnecessary tasks over and over again to ensure there was nothing outstanding that could be the instigator of discipline or direction. Making sure you remain completely silent when the ice cream man comes around because asking for something other than the immediate necessities of food, water and shelter would be deemed unacceptable. Hiding away the school trip forms that might cost money or being genuinely terrified about bringing letters home that required some sort of action or something that might incur a level of stress or deliberation beyond the norm. Being impeccably behaved in and around school and out of school to make sure I attracted no unnecessary attention. The one thing I stood up for throughout my childhood, the one thing I fought for was the time and transport needed to go and play football. Football was like a bloody religion to me as a child and I would have walked the 7 miles to and from the training ground should it have been necessary. But even the simple task of ensuring your daughter attended football training safely was too much of a request most of the time. Asking for a 15-minute lift to football matches was like asking my parent to drive me to complete a drug deal in another fucking continent. I soon ended up just being in the backseat of all my mates' parents' cars and they were always more than happy to drive me. Being the only girl amongst a football team of lads, holding my own (and then some) on the pitch every week and not having a supportive parent of my own on the side-lines, meant most other parents developed quite a soft spot for me.

I thrived on football as a kid. I absolutely lived and breathed it and I was determined not to let my doggedly discouraging parent stop me from doing what I loved. I must have been about 11 years old when I broke my arm playing football with a group of lads on a Sunday morning. I sustained the injury through stopping the shot of a bloke triple my age and was more than happy to take the risk of breaking a bone, just to ensure I didn't let his powerful effort go past me. Safe to say, his mates absolutely ripped the piss out of him when I made a brilliant save to keep his shot out as they continually rubbed salt in his wound by showering me with praise. As proud as I was to have saved the middle-aged bloke's near-certain goal, the pain of my broken bone hit instantly. Knowing what I'd face when I got home with the inconvenience of an injury, I seriously considered covering it up for as long as I could cope with because the resulting trip to hospital would have inevitably caused more discomfort than it was worth, irrelevant of the broken bone. The near-immediate bruising and swelling around my left arm were too much to cover up and too painful to bear for much longer, so I plucked up the courage to ask my mother for a lift to the hospital. Instead of a sympathetic cuddle and some frozen peas (which a fucking stranger would have offered, let alone your own parent) I was marched over to the next-door neighbour (who was a nurse) to ascertain whether it was worth her time taking me to hospital or whether I was just making a fuss. I was literally silent, clasping on to my swollen arm, by the way – there are kids that would have made more fuss having their hair cut than I made with a broken bone. And just for the record – the bloke with a white stick, glasses and a guide dog could have told you it was broken, but the increasing swelling and bruising wasn't enough for her, it had to be clarified I was worthwhile enough to be taken to hospital. Obviously, the neighbour advised straight away I, at the very least, go and get it looked at and so began the very short 10-

minute drive to the hospital where I was berated for at least 9 of them. Would you Adam and Eve it? My arm was broken and needed a cast and I gained a completely warped, nonsensical feeling of satisfaction that my near non-existent fuss was justified. After the usual scolding because my broken bone had inconvenienced her, the sympathy and maternal facade returned when the doctors were present and on the very quiet journey home. It would appear that I could never, ever please my mother and anything I did above and beyond the realms of a normal child, seemed to go completely unnoticed. Maybe they were noticed and hell, even appreciated but she just wasn't sure how to show that. I'm grateful for my mother; she taught me a great deal. I'm sure your husband having an 18-month affair, secretly having another baby and leaving you with 2 children under the age of 10 would be enough to tip anyone over the edge. But my brother and I were the ones being crushed at the bottom when she was tipped over the edge and fell to the bottom. My childhood (or complete lack of it) contributed significantly to very nearly coming to a premature end.

Football was the light at the end of the tunnel of so many days in my childhood and my grandad soon took responsibility for chauffeuring me around the country for training and matches and I'm still not sure to this day who loved it more. We would spend hours in the car, sometimes travelling the length and breadth of the country, and that man knew the UK roads better than any satellite navigation system available. It was as much of a joy for him as it was for me and his palpable enthusiasm in standing on the side-lines, chatting to all the other dads, dissecting every move of the game on the way home and having a good old rant about the terrible refereeing decisions was not only completely infectious, it was a revelation to me. He loved taking me to football; he looked forward to it like I did. It was *our* time and *our* passion. For a man brought up in a generation where all women were good for was cooking and cleaning, his passion for the woman's game was astounding. Nothing was ever too much for my grandad and if we had to leave at 6pm, he'd be ready at the door by 5:30. If we had to drive to Wales (which we did for an under 15 England camp at Lilleshall), he'd book a B and B and make best friends with the owner. He cared as much for my friends in the team and their wellbeing as I did. The friendships forged throughout a childhood chasing football dreams and ambitions tend to last a very, very long time. You spend your weekends and 2 nights a week with these young women who all have the same interests and ambitions as you. Our women's football team was closer to a sisterhood – as it should have been. You have each other's backs and would put in a shift for them on or off the pitch – no questions asked. These friendships are maintained even if (and when) football careers start to dwindle later in life. Football, the friends it gave me that I held so dear and the time it gave me with my grandad was, without doubt, the very best part of my childhood and adolescence. So, it was an unspeakably tragic day when a completely unexpected and horrible accident turned that positive football bubble inside out.

I was a goalkeeper in my football career (which is ironic considering I struggle to stand still for five minutes nowadays) and it is a well-known fact that goalkeeping is a hugely unique position in the beautiful game. You can go from an adrenaline-fuelled one on one standoff with a 6ft-tall brute of a striker, to taking a ball straight in the face from point-blank range, to plucking the ball from mid-air from a swirling cross in the afternoon wind. Then, in some games, you may not touch the ball for 89 minutes but you are expected to maintain your concentration in order pull off a top corner wonder save in the last kick of the game, to save your team 3 points. You needed the concentration, agility, courage and timing of a wild animal catching its prey and the list of very specific attributes required to be successful between the sticks didn't stop there. You have to be independent, brave, committed, commanding, confident, self-assured, consistent, reliable and a bit of a 'gob shite.' No, that's wrong. You have to be a huge 'gob shite.' You also had to have more than 1 screw slightly loose to actually choose to be the last line of defence between the net and a constant barrage of well-struck spheres of leather. This was very handy because my goalkeeping partner and friend, Sian and I, happened to have all of those qualities in abundance. We had a full toolbox, full of loose screws between us. Sian was the most fantastic character and could light up a dank and dingy Sunday morning changing room just by walking into it. Throughout our teenage years, we would train together every week, comparing our new pairs of gloves and relentlessly taking the piss out of our poor goalkeeping coaches. We would applaud one another when we had pulled off a seemingly unreachable tip over the bar or gave a consoling pat on the head when we let the odd one slip through our legs. We shared countless 90-minute games playing 45 minutes each and working out what we'd both done well and what needed improving. We were both fantastic footballers and helped each other master our passion. It wasn't just me that welcomed and appreciated Sian's company and humour; it was the whole team. Sian was the sort of person you were so proud to have as a friend and one you knew would give as good as she got. She was never afraid to say how she felt and she undoubtedly had the right balance of confidence and self-belief to go far in the women's game.

We were training twice a week during pre-season training for the 09-10 season in Ipswich on a Tuesday and Thursday evening. We would all congregate in the late evening sun, wondering how much of a thrashing we'd be getting for 2 solid hours to prepare us for the season ahead. It was Thursday 14th August 2009 and, as goalkeepers, we were always given the luxury of choosing what type of training we would be doing. The decision was between choosing to go and smash out some specific goalkeeping-based drills, handling or ball work whilst the outfield players are being run ragged. Or, join in with the outfield players' lung-busting drills as a goalkeeper required a certain level of speed and anaerobic ability too. I'd usually choose ball work over running back then; there was nothing I loved more than getting my body in the way of a well-struck football, but that night I chose to run. I was in need of a good energy-sapping session and whilst I went off and ran, Sian did the handling drills with our coach which we would have usually done together. I chose not to have that precious 20 minutes together that evening, chatting complete nonsense and focussing intently on not dropping the ball. I chose to run instead and that decision still plays on my mind to this day. Four days after that training session on Monday 17th August 2009, our tightly knit team, with even tighter friendships, was torn apart. On that evening, Sian had been involved in a terrible, fatal accident where the car she was travelling in hit a sign on the near side carriageway of the A14 and she tragically died at the scene.

My coach at the time had the awful task of phoning each and every one of the team and telling them what had happened. I can remember the exact moment I heard the news and remember being in a complete state of confusion. I couldn't comprehend at all what had happened and was convinced it wasn't real. The brutal realisation that it was the truth soon followed and I was completely inconsolable, as was the whole team. I sobbed and sobbed for days and was still in complete shock weeks after that horrible night. About a week or so after Sian's death, it was decided that we should play our scheduled fixture on the Sunday afternoon to honour Sian as it would have undoubtedly been what she wanted. The entirety of her incredible family came to watch the game that day and it was the bravest display of family unity I'd ever seen. Dedicated t-shirts were made for Sian with a gorgeous picture of her on the front and we all wore them with pride throughout the warm-up, as did most of her family as well. Everywhere you looked on the pitch throughout the warm-up there was a player with Sian's face lighting up their torso. It struck me in almost the first minute of the game that the whole family must have been looking at me stood in between the goalposts longing for their daughter, sister, niece or aunty to be standing in the place I was. I was overcome with a sense of guilt that the wrong goalkeeper was taken. The wrong one was now standing in this place. Sian was full of life with a huge, extended network of supportive family and loyal friends. She had potential, she had the world at her feet and I was standing there instead of her. I couldn't shift the idea that my pathetic existence had outlived hers which, to me, had such a greater meaning and purpose than the life I was desperately clinging on to. My plans to commit suicide were already manifesting themselves and I had the audacity to be stood here when a much better young woman had been taken from us? It was all so wrong. Committing suicide wouldn't have brought Sian back; it would have taken away my feelings of guilt but only caused more despair for all involved. So, it was apparent my adolescent self-indulgence was already shamefully coming to the surface even then. Part of the reasoning behind me wanting to commit suicide was because I had such a feeling of guilt that another young precious life had been taken, that wasn't mine, yet I thought it should have been. It makes absolutely no sense now, even reading it in black and white, so there was no way I was going to be able to deconstruct it and deal with it in my already chaotic teenage brain at that time.

The relationship I have with Sian's family to this day is like that of an adopted daughter. Our shared commitment to one another throughout life's atrocities has created a long-lasting connection that I genuinely don't think could be broken by anything. Our experiences together really do trump that of even the most adverse family life events and inevitably that has made them and I stronger as both a unit and individuals. Sian's mother, Chrissie, is one of the most stoical women I know and she has quite evidently passed this trait on to her children. Of course, she and her family would have given literally anything to see Sian standing in between the sticks, commanding her six-yard area with the effortless nature she conducted herself with in all sports. But that did not mean for one second that they wished she was there *instead* of me. My irrational thoughts that I was far more worthy of death than Sian were just that, entirely irrational. But they were thoughts that governed my mind for months and months after her death. Chrissie and her family were, in fact, a radiant beacon of light for the whole of the football team, operating an open-door policy to anyone who was struggling, whether they had known Sian for years or a matter of moments. I grabbed this opportunity with open arms and immersed myself in that family's infectious togetherness and unity. There is an immense feeling of pride both on my part (and I hope) as well as theirs, that despite the fact Sian's death contributed, in part, to my psychological downward spiral, her family have been one of the biggest contributors to my recovery. There is nothing that could impact on that family now that isn't 100 times easier than what they haven't already been through. Becoming a part of their family unit gave me a hugely significant element of my life I didn't even realise I had been missing. They gave me that indescribable, rare, *family* part of life that welcomes you and allows you into a buzzing, happily drunken kitchen at 3am, participating in incredibly intense games of Articulate, but also facilitates a 'quiet cup of tea and biscuits' afternoon when you need some maternal guidance or a comfy shoulder to lean on. That was a part of life I hadn't experienced properly until I was welcomed into that family. The Ryan's were a family in every single sense of the word and it was extended to every corner possible. I couldn't have felt more a part of it and I absorbed all the love and warm embraces I could from that house, and very much still do, as did everyone that set foot in it.

There was no real front runner that contributed to my decision on the 12th November 2010, no one thing that stood out as the reason I couldn't continue. The combination of the many significant life events I'd experienced before even turning 18 was enough to make me contemplate a permanent solution to a lot of temporary problems. But as soon as the notion of committing suicide entered my brain, I became totally obsessed with it. There was no other option from that moment on. It was my golden ticket out of what I had deemed to be a meaningless existence and I was not letting it go. I didn't even acknowledge the idea of a future once I had made the decision to take control in the only way I knew how. The road to my planned final destination of that lay-by at the side of the A14 was a pothole-covered, congested, roadwork-interrupted hellish journey, that had more than its fair share of bumps in the road. But the initial journey following that awful pit stop was not much easier either. However, I would never have wished for an easier path throughout my broken childhood, for it is often the most treacherous paths that lead to the most glorious locations. Right now, I'd consider myself sitting in one of those glorious locations, enjoying a flask of tea and a shortbread biscuit. A few less potholes to dig my way out of would have been nice, but I wouldn't change a single thing about my past and no one else should wish to change their own personal tapestry either. Your past and the experiences within it are what build your character and the sort of person you are. The bricks that have been left outside exposed to all the elements for months and months before they go on to build a house, will weather the inevitable storm a lot easier when it comes in the future. The bricks that have only known warmth and protection from the elements before they go on to build a house, may well still create the structure, but will not know what has hit them when they have to weather their first storm.

Chapter 7.

A Very Long Weekend in Chile

"What the hell is that bloke doing? I cannot believe he is doing it like that!"

"She is making that look a lot harder than it actually is. I could do that with my eyes closed. This is cringe-worthy; where do they find these people?"

"That's it. I can't watch this bloody rubbish anymore. Change the channel – they are all pathetic!"

We have all done it. We have all been guilty of it. Sitting clutching a glass of vino, nestled nicely into our DFS sale sofa, tucking into our third bowl of bacon frazzles, criticising some poor sod on the latest reality television series. Nonchalantly mocking their poor attempts at starting their own business, baking a cake, reinventing the wheel, skating in diamond-encrusted ill-fitting lycra, teaching their dog a foreign language, sewing a wetsuit for the new gender-neutral Barbie doll or whatever other ridiculous concept that particular channel was trying to flog. That is, of course, what makes reality television so inviting in all of its weird and wonderful forms. It is entirely relatable to every Tom, Dick, Harry or whoever else plonks themselves down in front of the box at 8pm, hoping for some entertaining distraction from everyday life. Who then, ironically, chooses to watch every other, slightly more ambitious Tom, Dick or Harry from everyday life complete rather extraordinary endeavours for a financial reward, show-biz contract or maybe just pure pride? Quite frankly, I'd had enough of insulting all of the individuals out there at least attempting to better themselves in some way. Whether by burning their seeded cob loaf, having their CV ripped apart in front of thousands, or shagging anything with a pulse in exchange for a 2-week all-inclusive in a beautiful foreign country. It was time to have a crack myself.

SAS: Who Dares Wins adopts a slightly different approach when it comes to conforming to the stereotypical 'reality show' procedures. Granted, it takes normal, everyday people and envelopes them in an unpredictable environment, chucks in a few demanding tasks and films it, in all its glory, for the gasping masses to drool over when it finally gets aired back home. But, the main premise of the show is to also replicate as closely as possible one of the most brutal military selection processes in the world. It is probably the only reality show that asks you to sign a disclaimer and insurance document before filming essentially explaining, if you die whilst participating in the show, well, no one forced you to participate, if you croak it, that's your problem. For those who have not seen it, the show itself is very simple. The production and editing staff go through a 6-month long audition process to find 25 recruits (from 2018 the show auditioned for male and female participants, the 3 series before 2018 included only male participants).These individuals came from every walk of life and every demographic in the UK, from poverty-soaked cobbled streets to 2-mile long driveways with a concierge at the door. The recruits, typically with no military background whatsoever are then thrown into a condensed selection programme simulating the near exact training a qualified soldier would experience if they were applying to join either the Special Air Service (SAS) or the Special Boat Service (SBS).

In its entirety in the real world, it is a 6-month long military course where professional soldiers require at least 2 years' experience before even applying. It attracts a plethora of highly qualified soldiers often with either Paratrooper or Marine experience to apply and still the average final pass rate is less than 10%. The training could include but was not limited to, sleep deprivation, exposure to heights, exposure to extreme physical exertion, exposure to extreme temperatures, insufficient food supplies, interrogation, stress positions, high altitude, limited sanitation, basic accommodation and repetitive intense psychological stress. Pah! I'm sure I've read holiday brochures that read worse than that. It will be just like a rather severe camping trip. Each recruit is given a numbered armband and that number is what they are lovingly referred to throughout the process. You were a number throughout, not a name. There were 2 ways to leave the course. Should the extremes of the experience become too much for an individual, they could, at any time 'VW.' Grab a complimentary Volkswagen and go home. Not really. VW stood for Voluntary Withdrawal, whereby simply handing your numbered armband into the Directing Staff (DS) and saying those crucial 2 words, would be enough to withdraw yourself from the course. The other method of getting yourself out of the hellish pit you voluntarily chose to jump into was to be culled by the DS for either being, in their professional opinion, too physically or psychologically weak to continue. I didn't let either of those outcomes so much as cross my busy little mind. If I say I am going to do something, come hell or high water, I'm going to do it; I'm going to commit my mind, body and soul to it.

I had been actively seeking the next challenge to keep me occupied after completing my first half Ironman in 2018. I had finished the recovery stage from that endeavour and needed my next purpose, my next focus. I remember being totally engrossed in the first 3 series of the programme. And definitely guilty of a few sofa-bound comments,

"I could do that; what are these imbeciles doing?"

The year of my application, 2018, was slightly more special. In 2018, for the first time ever, the Ministry of Defence opened up all 'Front Line' military roles to women. Before this compelling and fantastically progressive decision, applying to be in either the SAS or SBS was out of bounds for female applicants in a genuine army environment and the spin-off reality show. So obviously, maintaining their accuracy to the process, in 2018 the producers of SAS: Who Dares Wins, for the first time ever, opened applications to the show up to women as well. There was absolutely no way I was not going to apply.

The application form itself was bold and precocious in what it asked of you. A distinctive, well-known part of the show is the mirror room interrogations where recruits are encouraged to delve into their past and regurgitate harrowing memories or experiences, that may have contributed to their decision to engage in something as ruthless and barbaric as the programme. So, without question, I eloquently detailed all over my form the tragic loss of George the hamster at just 6 years old and how this horrifying event shaped the rest of my life, my philosophies and my 100% vegan lifestyle... Did I bollocks. I was honest and articulately explained every inch of my past in great detail. This was an unmissable opportunity to take more responsibility for my past and use it as a positive foundation to help myself and others. To not take full advantage of this moment landing in my lap would be senseless. Walked out in front of a lorry a few years ago and then I have the opportunity to embark on one of the most physically and psychologically demanding military selection processes in the world which has the added bonus of being plastered all over national television?? Sign me up, buttercup.

The actual audition process was fascinating. I had to travel down to London on numerous occasions for fitness tests, heart scans, face to face interviews, vaccinations and meetings. Being invited to the Centre for Health and Human Performance on Harley Street, to delicately test my lung capacity in a VO2 max test, was a particular honour considering the huge exercise geek that I am. That enlightening experience was, however, months down the line in the recruitment process. It all started with a fitness testing day in Camden and walking in to the secondary school where the day was taking place was literally like walking in to 'Body Builders Anonymous.' I was engulfed in an uncomfortable, sweaty sandwich of biceps and pecs, bursting out of vests that would have looked oversized on a 7-year-old. Men and women that quite clearly spend 26 hours a day locked in the gym but more than likely have the personality of a paper clip filled every corner of the building.

Even then I knew that this programme had very little to do with physical fitness but apparently these other people didn't. Yes, having the ability to lift heavy and run long and fast in this process would be beneficial to an extent. But what it would take to survive in the environment we were signing up for was nearly entirely psychological. It required stoicism and the ability to endure physical 'beastings' with a quietly confident, resilient and positive mindset. It required the ability to undertake hugely demanding physical tasks and not have someone caress your ego the entire time. It required the motivation to complete something entirely for a personal sense of pride and accomplishment not a pat on the back. It required deep-rooted, internal motivation to tolerate the harshest of conditions because you have enough perspective to see the bigger picture and understand that exposure to discomfort will not only build you and better you, but also won't last forever. It required simple, psychological resilience and an appreciation that adversity will inevitably only create long term personal qualities that underpin success and progression.

I took immense pride in the fact I beat 'Beatrice Biceps' in the bleep test and gave a good account of myself across the board of fitness tests on the day. I'd barely caught my breath before they hauled me in for my filmed interview. When you consider there were upwards of 500 people there on just that one day, being chosen first for an interview could only have been a good thing. I reeled off the most comprehensive answers I could to their increasingly intimate questions and even had to show off my impressive scars for the camera. Surely a good old-fashioned scar and suicide sob story will get me my coveted place on Series 4. Maybe I shouldn't have been so self-deprecating, whether it was my scar, my story, my resilience or my terrible sense of humour, a few weeks and a couple more meetings later, I WAS IN. Out of 25,000 applicants I was to be one of the 25 recruits chosen to be on series 4 of this very well-known reality television programme. Sorry Naked Attraction, I'll have to take you up on your offer another year.

If you've come this far into the book you will probably have established (for more than a few pages) I'm a bit of a gob shite, so having to keep this new bit of news a secret was beyond difficult. I had to have a mysterious 2 weeks off from work and try and disappear out of the country for while without creating too much suspicion. The location of where we were actually going for our glamorous all-inclusive holiday wasn't revealed until the day before we flew out there. The previous series had either been in the dusty heat of the Moroccan desert, the unforgiving humidity of the Ecuadorian jungle or the bleak, wintery conditions of the Brecon Beacons. A quiet little Caribbean island, dusted with golden sand and plump coconuts would have suited me down to a tee. No such luck. We were heading to Chile in South America to battle with the high altitude, but be in awe of the stunning beauty of the Andes Mountains. Get me on that 14-hour flight. I was so ready to take this next challenge on.

The other 24 recruits were all huddled in the busy Heathrow airport but we were strictly told not to have too much communication with each other. That didn't faze me too much as I was too focussed already, I wasn't there to make friends (an attitude which I would later live to regret). I was there to let this new challenge develop attributes I hopefully never knew I had. The secrecy and lack of communication we became accustomed to from the outset became a prominent feature throughout the whole experience. From hour to hour, you never really knew what was coming or what was around the corner. It was literally an on-looking psychologist's wet dream. Imagine observing a bunch of over-confident, expectant, egotistical individuals walking into the complete unknown and having their backside handed to them on a plate. All of us were also, slowly but surely, trying to compete with the rising anxiety levels that we were all desperately trying to mask.

Typically, when you are going to be functioning in a high-altitude environment for a prolonged period of time, you gradually take 2-3 weeks to acclimatise to the conditions and allow your body to be accustomed to the much greater demand it would be under. We didn't have 2-3 weeks, we had 1 day. Fresh off a 14-hour flight and still totally bemused as to when the actual process would be starting, we were bundled into a minibus and driven up the most beautiful mountain Chile had to offer. Admittedly, I'm not that well-travelled but our journey up to the top was reminiscent of the scene from the original Italian Job film, where the coach meanders its way higher and higher up the side of a gargantuan spectacle with the views becoming more and more breath-taking the higher you go. There were tiny little cabins perched on the edge of the road which had probably not been inhabited for decades. Their historic presence was quickly being consumed by the small skiing centres that were cropping up around every corner too, attracting all sorts of tourists donned in brightly coloured puffer jackets. At that point, we were only half an hour or so from the capital of Chile, Santiago, so tourists and holidaymakers were a frequent occurrence. This was a world away from what we were about to be thrown into. This was merely a mild 24-hour practice run.

We were hauled out onto a vast rocky expanse looking out over ridges and peaks of mountain ranges.

The particular ridge to the right of where we were gathered had its own rather impressive incline. The temporary instructor was actually one of the course doctors who had the unenviable task of leading this dress rehearsal to try and prepare us for what we would be experiencing in the next few days.

"Right, shut up and listen. All of you, run as fast as you can to that far rock over there, do ten press-ups and run back."

Really, Doc? Is that the best you can do? That is barely even a warm-up for us fitness enthusiasts. Easypeasy. We will all annihilate that small task in seconds and be back begging for a far more onerous one.

"GO!!"

'Jesus Christ. What the hell has happened to my lungs?'

My brain was completely dumbfounded as I'd run 50 yards and was gasping for air. My pathetic little lungs had shrivelled up and were apparently performing like that of an 80-year-old lifelong smoker with a cracking case of bronchitis. Ah, I soon realised what was happening. Hello, altitude, how lovely of you to pop along and cuddle my lungs like a sodding Boa Constrictor. The best way I've ever heard exercising at altitude described is like when you have been underwater for 5 seconds too long and it's that exact moment you emerge from the water in a wild panic and can barely get your breath.

When you've been stuck under some dickhead's inflatable flamingo in a crowded holiday swimming pool, and then finally reach the surface, almost passing out because of the oxygen deprivation. Well, we were stuck under a thousand bloody flamingos out there. This was the first physiological hurdle to overcome. After no more than half an hour of impossibly demanding hill sprints, very poor press-ups and our lungs falling out of arse, we were back down the mountain to the gorgeous hotel you certainly would not associate with military training. But we hadn't even started yet; not even close.

The 4:30am wakeup call the next morning was edging slightly closer to the conditions I was expecting, but I knew this would definitely be the last time I was gently stretching out in Egyptian cotton sheets for a while. Still, the anxiety was simmering. I was half expecting a 6 ft tall, balaclava-wearing thug to ambush me at the fruit section of the breakfast spread. But I'm not entirely sure that would have given off the correct impression in the final edit. After stomaching as many eggs and bacon as possible (I had no idea what we would be living off for the next few days), our very limited stash of personal belongings was taken from us and piled into a separate vehicle to the one we were getting into. We were unreliably told that the vehicle was taking our bags to a hotel closer to the actual filming site and we were heading out on one more acclimatisation exercise before the process was due to begin the following morning. And just like the foolish, unsuspecting little idiot I am, I believed every word. So did every other recruit by the looks of things.

So, there we all went, scurrying off into another coach that looked like it hadn't passed an MOT since 1986, slightly more composed knowing our EXACT itinerary for the day. Deeper and deeper we drove into the mountainous surroundings. I felt so insignificant amongst the beautiful snow-dipped peaks that covered every corner of the landscape. They were strikingly beautiful yet fiercely ominous at the same time. I continued to gaze out of the window like some sort of gobsmacked tourist, safe in the knowledge we were just heading out for another gentle session and snuggling into a safe hotel later that night. However, the further we travelled into the desolate surroundings, the less sure I felt that a £50 a night Travelodge would appear balancing on the side of one of the many mountain edges.

Within seconds of questioning my hotel hypothesis, the white backdrop of the morning sky was suddenly illuminated with a sharp, rising flame coming from the front of the coach.

BANG!!

The ferocious flame was accompanied by a terrific noise and I could feel the heat, even at the very back of the vehicle.

"Jesus Christ. This shit heap has finally given out on us."

Even at that point, I hadn't even contemplated that this was the big ambush I had previously been mocking. It wasn't until I was being violently grabbed by the scruff of the neck and hauled out of my seat, whilst being screamed at for lifting my head so much as an inch that I realised, maybe we weren't headed for a hotel. This was it. My real SAS experience had begun in the most spectacular fashion.

Being marched across uneven rocks and shoved down into the snow wasn't as spectacular and I could instantly feel the cold flush through my system as we were made to kneel, motionless in the snow for what felt like a solid half an hour. Obviously, as soon as we were kneeling in stony silence, contemplating the horror that awaited us as we were about to embark on the most brutal few days of our life – someone farted. Holding back a nervous giggle is challenging at the best of times, but with 4 ex-SAS and SBS soldiers breathing down my neck, I knew cracking a smile at that precise moment would have landed me (and the many others holding back a chuckle) in a world of trouble. Before Captain Farty Pants could let rip again, our first physical task was thrown upon us as one of the DS went sprinting off into the mountainous backdrop and we were politely ordered to catch him (or just chase him in my case).

That inconvenient Boa Constrictor was soon back to visit my lungs as all 25 of us navigated the rockiest terrain I'd ever run across. I was running past 2 if not 3 other recruits that had absolutely slammed face-first into the deck after losing their footing on one of the copious rugged rocks cluttering our path. 'This is not the time to be getting a sprained ankle,' I thought as I sat in the middle of the pack, already trying to give a good account of myself.

"STOP FUCKING CRUISING, YOU IN THE BURGUNDY HOODY!!"

I was quite impressed at the detailed colour description from the DS of one of my old, tattered hoodies, but didn't have the energy or the audacity to reply and explain I was literally giving everything and we were 20 minutes in. That was the sort of psychological humiliation that just became a staple throughout. Little digs at your performance, your commitment, your appearance, or just who you were as a person. It was all part of the mind games. They expected utter perfection from you and any slight deviation from that was picked up on. I was more than accustomed to verbal, direct and indirect physical abuse by now so I didn't let anything in. Any insult, any degrading comment, anything at all, I just put my trusty shield up and let the words bounce off (as I typically do in life); I had bigger fish to fry.

After a few more minutes in a very shaky press-up hold and an endless reverse plank at the finish line of the rocky road run, the first arduous physical task was done. I noticed the red raw skin already beginning to protrude on the palms of my hands from the contact with the stony surface beneath us and at just the same time, I also noticed the unmistakable stench of urine beginning to emanate throughout the truck. Recruit number 17 had openly admitted to wetting herself during the run. She was desperate, and believe it or not, there were not many public conveniences where we were. This was the bizarre normality that we all had to very quickly adapt to. A sense of camaraderie was already beginning to build as we trundled along in the military vehicles transporting us to our 5-star accommodation. I still chose to keep myself to myself and not partake in the gentle banter being thrown around throughout the uncomfortable journey. As I picked at the broken skin on the palms of my hands, I knew we still had a very long way to go.

After plenty more 'Italian Job' moments with the slightly erratic truck driver, we pulled up to what we would be calling home for the next few days. I had never viewed anywhere so bleak but so stunning at the same time. The old mining camp was encased by snow-dusted mountains and pure white glaciers. There was a distinct feeling that this bit of the world hadn't seen human life for at least 50 years and the mountains were disgruntled we were now stepping on their territory. The pearly tips of the mountains blended in with the pure white of the sky; it consistently looked as if it was about to dump 2 years' worth of snow on us at any given moment. The corrugated iron, oblong, army green cabins were not in keeping at all with the beautiful aesthetic that surrounded them. The toilets consisted of a row of 5 wooden cubicles, with battered, wooden swinging doors like the old western movies. The doors covered just your midriff at a push, forget keeping your modesty with any other part of your body. Each cubicle had a wooden seat with a circular hole cut into it, sitting on top of an old, hollow oil tank that would house our piss and shit for a couple of days, before the stench got too much and we were ordered to steadily lift them out and burn the contents, before placing them back again. To say the accommodation was basic would have actually been a compliment. I don't think there are many humans from the Western world who can say they have ever experienced poor sanitation. I was immediately humbled to be able to say that I'd spent 27 years of my life with a flushing toilet – I still think it is a privilege we take for granted. It was refreshing to be taken back to the very bare basics, and I guarantee you, there was no toilet in the world that had a better view than this one. My usual view from my home toilet is a charming, if slightly tacky, picture of Marilyn Monroe, intently watching as I let nature take its course. In Chile, I was peering out over one of the most breath-taking mountain ranges I'd ever seen, wondering whether my piss would instantly freeze the minute it hit the air, with a fully grown bloke sitting inches away from me curling one out without a care in the world.

Even from my very, very limited experience of military life, SAS: WDW gave me an opportunity to relate to so many serving soldiers who crave a military existence when they are back on 'Civvy Street.' There is an alluring simplicity to military life, where, despite the fact you may be engulfed in fatal firefights, be just metres away from bombs exploding, or literally stare death in the face around every corner, there is such peace in the way of life. There are no phones, no emails, no social media, no condescending and meaningless distractions, no post, bills or letters to deal with, life admin is uncomplicated and it's black and white. You know what is expected from you and as long as your shit is squared away, you don't have to worry about wiping the arse or holding the hand of anyone else. This experience was inevitably going to be ruthless but it was also a complete privilege to be there. As more splinters penetrated my arse cheek on the next toilet trip, I looked out on my temporary home and instead of apprehending more psychological or physical affliction, I embraced every single second. What a time to be alive.

Within the luxury accommodation were 25 camping beds, each one with a canvas covering supposed to hold your entire body weight, so thin it was almost transparent. The glorified doormats (I can't bring myself to call it a bed again) were all laid out next to each other, with individual green military Bergens placed at the end of each one. I happily took on the military precision and uniformity we were being engulfed in. We were all in the same boat, we all looked the same, ate the same, slept the same and carried the same weight. Considerable controversy arose around the decision to include women in the fourth series (as well as in real military front-line roles) as to whether they would be carrying the same weight as the men. Of course we bloody were and it should never be any different. I hadn't chosen to throw myself into one of the most intense military selection courses in the world to have exceptions made because of what is in between my legs. Each and every one of us carried 25kg in our Bergens and it was your individual responsibility to measure it with exact military precision. If you put too many sandbags in and you weighed in at over 25kg – good luck, you've just personally and directly made your life a lot harder. Come in under 25kg – you had to go and get the biggest rock you could find and put it in your Bergen. Ensuring the most basic of tasks were done correctly and with the utmost exactitude became completely paramount. In the real military world, perfection in every task you undertake could literally be the difference between life and death. Male or female, you had to conduct yourself in the most meticulous manner. The only thing that could differentiate us all was our physical and psychological attitude which was again about to be tested.

After kitting us out in really, really comfortable khaki trousers, long-sleeved tops and incomprehensibly heavy boots, we were out running (I can't speak for everyone else but I was closer to sprinting), again to another unknown destination. You never, ever knew what was round the corner. The sofa-dweller's favourite question would often be,

"So, do they tell you what you are about to do, prep you, brief you, dust you down, do your make up and then turn the cameras on??"

In a word: no. The cameras were rolling 24-7 and you didn't know if you were about to jump out of a helicopter or carry a fully grown man on your shoulder up an icy mountain. The next task was sort of a combination of both. The directing staff made the demonstration look easy. We were all intently watching on as one DS abseiled down a small rock face and jumped into an icy cold waterfall whilst the other asked him to recall the name of his siblings at the same time as dealing with the shock of the water. He was then required to submerge himself into the bitter cold river once more until being told to come to the surface again. As soon as I stepped into the waterfall, the frosty water filled my boots, legs and then torso as I tried to take control of my breathing. Attempting to keep calm whilst icy water floods your clothes and body is like asking a Spanish bull to relax at a Simply Red concert. The rocky terrain underfoot was not making gradually stepping into the water any easier, but, speaking from experience, I believe cold water is like ripping off a plaster; you've got to take a deep breath and get it done as swiftly as possible. I successfully recalled the names of all 4 of my siblings and hauled myself out of the beautiful but utterly piercing waterfall.

Again, absolutely no questions were asked when both male and female recruits were stripping down until they were stark bollock naked in the crowded but wonderfully warm tent. The priority wasn't really working out whose testicle was staring you in the face, more getting the sodden kit off your shaking body and getting something dry on. I debated whether to remove my sports bra, as did many of the other female recruits. We had two sets of clothes, a wet kit and a dry kit. But we had one pair of pants and one bra. I could cope with going kamikaze for a few miles, but scurrying across mountainous terrain like a feral dog with no support for these bad boys? Not a chance. 32 bee stings or not, I could not run without a sports bra albeit a soggy, cold sports bra. This instantaneously became a prime opportunity for the chief DS to unashamedly highlight the male-female divide and what a huge burden the women were because the majority of us had chosen to keep on a wet piece of clothing. The fact we weren't given a spare and our performance would have undoubtedly been hampered without one, were nothing but pathetic excuses. But it was also a gentle nod to the realisation that producers have never had to cater to women on this show before. They just about managed 2 tampons in our welcome pack, never mind a thought to spare underwear. Our blatant incompetence and selfish attempt at mild comfort would (in any genuine warfare scenario) cause us to freeze to death and be an extra weight to carry. So, a brutal punishment was, of course, in order. A solid 30 minutes of holding our 25kg Bergens above our heads, combined with more sit-ups and press-ups using jagged stones as our gym mat and you could say that was a lesson firmly learnt. Found yourself with a wet sports bra in freezing conditions? Your instructions in that scenario were to (and I quote),

'Take the Fucker off.'

The chief course doctor, Sundeep, was a mild-mannered and conscientious man. He must have always been employing a delicate balancing act between keeping us all alive but not allowing us to feel an inch of compassion, or that he might give a shit if we were struggling to have a shit. Personally, I was the exact opposite and couldn't stop shitting. We'd been given in-depth lectures before venturing out to our abandoned accommodation about keeping hydrated, attacking everything we ate with a copious amount of salt, battling with the poor sanitation to not allow seemingly innocuous cuts and bruises to get infected and not moaning about any medical issues unless it was absolutely necessary. I'd been feeling dog rough from the moment we landed, but I was more than happy to attribute that to the severe change in altitude, extreme physical exertion, lack of sleep and general anxiety about what I was taking on. I 'assaulted' my cement-mixer porridge every morning just like everyone else and cracked on. Unless your head was falling off or you were bleeding profusely, you didn't have much scope to go and visit the Doc.

In my usual sadistic manner, I looked forward to the purely psychological challenges. The experiences where you knew you would be exposed to something, the vast majority would deem terrifying, distressing, uncomfortable or just so far detached from normality you wouldn't even allow it to concern you in routine existence. I thrived off those sorts of experiences. I had such trust in my mental resilience that I truly believed no psychological beating could derail me in the slightest. Another ankle-breaking trek across the local Chilean nature trails led us to the most colossal rock face this beautiful country had to offer. It was as though a deli counter worker had taken their cheese wire and split this monstrous rock completely in half, just leaving the flat, exposed, vertical face we were all gawping up at. The next requirement of us was to ascend this 70ft mass, crevice by crevice, not celebrate at all when finally reaching the top then FORWARD abseil down it. Forward abseil? Just when you think you can predict what is around the corner.... BAM! Special Forces selection training comes along and shatters your incorrect illusions.

We weren't taking the easy route. We weren't allowed the luxury of sitting comfortably and abseiling backwards down the rock face. We had to stand over the vertical drop and witness every single step of our own descent until the black dots at ground level eventually looked like human beings again. The view at the top of the monumental climb was simply breath-taking. I was enclosed yet again in an expanse of mountains that had evidently not been touched by human hand in decades. The flawless pearly peaks were camouflaged impeccably into the wintery sky. I was just about to pull out my binoculars for a spot of bird watching when I was ordered into position to begin my downward decline. I was struggling far more with the practicalities of actually roping yourself down a mountain than any associated fear that I was supposed to be feeling. The further you could hold the tightly wired rope out to your right and allow it to flow through your palm, the easier your descent would be. The rock face was gradually becoming greasier as it started to teem it down with rain just before my turn. It was a considerable height and I could certainly feel the positive correlation between the increasing palpitations in my chest and the decreasing number of inches to the cliff edge as I shuffled closer and closer. I wouldn't go as far as to say I was scared; I knew I was relatively safe. As much as watching a budding SAS recruit gallantly fall to their death descending a 70ft rock face might boost the ratings for that episode, safety was always paramount. I knew my fluctuating emotions would settle again once this minor task was over, so I momentarily shoved how I was feeling to the back of my mind and got on with it.

That was another great tool that I already possessed but honed even more throughout my SAS experience. Emotions are important things and should be embraced at every opportunity. I'll cry without fail at Mufasa's death on my 487th viewing of The Lion King, every single time, just like every other adult in the country. I'll forever blame it on hay-fever, to maintain my very confident and, at times, weirdly masculine outer layer. However, there are very specific occasions when emotions also need to be ignored and you have the power to do that. If you have the power to create this monumental fear inside your very own brain, then you also have the power to remove it, control it or just ignore it. It wasn't the rock that was adjusting my emotions, it wasn't the authoritative DS that caused a change in my outlook, I couldn't even blame the altitude this time; it was me and me alone. So, I chose to ignore my mild anxiety; I was absolutely not letting it get in the way of surmounting this obstacle. That was within my control. Just like it was my choice to allow the rock to throw me off track slightly, it was also my choice to get right back on it again and move forward. I acknowledged that I was pushing my already very permeable comfort zone and thrived off the adrenaline that was also now pumping through my veins. I needed to take control of my emotions for a maximum of ten minutes. I needed to ignore the anxiety I was responsible for creating for ten very small minutes. If we can command every emotion we create, entirely by ourselves, seemingly impossible tasks become doable. What makes something impossible? You are too scared to do it? (Fear). It is too expensive? (Self-Doubt). It is too far away? (Self-belief). Only a handful of people have done it before? (Despondency/Jealousy/Resentment). The only things determining whether something is impossible are you and your emotions and you have complete control over them.

Leaning over the top of the rock, the soles of my feet were now flush to the rock face. I was stood vertically on the flat rock face and felt a bit like Spider-Man with concussion. He really could scale walls and flat surfaces. I was already slipping and sliding down the descent like Bambi on ice. It was actually helpful every time I slipped or lost my footing. When I slipped, my brain's immediate reaction was,

"SHIT, I'M GOING TO FALL!"

So, every time I slipped and didn't fall, it soon trained my brain into realising I was safe and I latched onto the technique of running down the side of the rock face. As predicted, the descent took no more than a few minutes but there was a solid feeling of pride when, finally and ungracefully,I hit the floor. I didn't allow the overbearing task in front of me to take control, I took control and got the job done. Obviously, the jubilant mumbling amongst us was more than enough to piss off the DS and just as soon as we'd all reached the bottom of the rock face, they were finding another, slightly more snowy one, to absolutely beast us on.

My feet were sinking into the fresh white layers of snow like quicksand. Every step was sapping an unimaginable amount of energy out of the soles of my feet as I desperately tried to lift my other boot out of the icy hole it was trapped in. Getting myself up the near-vertical hill was hard enough, that was without transporting an 80kg male recruit on my back like an ill-fitting haversack. I trudged up to the top of the mini-mountain, my legs so burnt out they must have been on the verge of falling off. The temptation to sit on my arse at the peak of the climb, slide the whole way down and scream, "WEEEEEEEEEEEEEEEEEEEE!!!!!!" at the top of my lungs was very distracting.

Thankfully, I didn't give in to temptation and after a few more snowy hill sprints, the 'beasting' was finally over. Every one of us, cold, wet and exhausted, slumped down in the military trucks waiting for us, hoping there would be no more unexpected interruptions and we could be still and rest for the journey back to base at the very least. Deep into those very rare quiet moments, it was difficult not to succumb to overthinking. I think being thrashed up and down a giant ice cube was probably easier to deal with, because your mind was occupied with where the next gasp of oxygen was coming from and nothing else. There were no limiting thoughts worming their way in, planting seeds of doubt in the grey matter that had, literally just an hour previous, guided you head-first down a sheer rock face.

"Stop it, Laura."

I had to snap myself out of the negative mindset as quickly as I had allowed myself to fall into it.

"You are good enough to be here. You deserve to be here. You do not feel as ill as you think you do. Get your head down, sleep and deal with whatever is coming next, when it comes."

The next day, we were dropped slap bang in the middle of the Las Aminas Hills. Firstly, whoever named it 'Hills' was having a laugh. An incredible landscape just on the North West coast of Chile, it was home to the sort of hills you had to arch your neck to see, like you were in the very front row of the cinema. It was another gloriously mountainous backdrop for us to firmly get our teeth into. Our task, as a team of 9, was to carry a 90kg log and two 10kg tyres (along with all our individual 25kgBergens) for 5 km up a steady incline across one of the aforementioned 'hills.' The equipment was supposed to replicate artillery that we would have to move across all sorts of terrain if this were the real deal. The log was just that. The real deal. No frills, no spills. A great solid log with no convenient handles to hold on to, no handy little straps to attach it to our back. Just a continuous, cylindrical hunk of wood that we had to transport, one way or another, up the bloody great hill. I had been nominated as second in command for this task, behind the leader for the task, recruit number 20.

Recruit 20 instantly made an impact on anyone the moment you looked at her, due to the small teardrop tattooed on the side of her face. In my own personal urban dictionary, that sort of tattoo stood for the fact you had murdered someone, but apparently, it was meant to represent the pain and suffering she had endured as a child. That small amount of ink under her left eye, or more significantly what it represented, instantly meant we got off on the wrong foot as it contradicts every single value and opinion I stand for. Our future is not governed by our past in any way, shape or form unless we allow it to be. If you don't take responsibility for your past and everything that has occurred within it, you are the only one who is going to suffer and you are the only one to blame for that suffering. Unfortunately, recruit 20 lived solidly in the past and blamed most, if not all, of her negative personality traits on that. She was entitled, selfish, powerless, and unjustifiably opinionated. She had a problem with the world and everyone in it and they had a problem back according to her. The world owed her absolutely everything because of what she had suffered as a child. She was like a Brillo pad; harsh, unwelcoming and aggressive. I have no doubt at all that her past was completely awful, harrowing and I wouldn't wish such an experience on any individual. But every single person in that process had some horrific demon in their closet. Bereavement, physical abuse, sexual abuse, neglect, bullying, alcoholism, drugs, violence, suffering, homelessness, and suicide to name just a few - the list was both utterly traumatic and unfortunately endless. Most could open the door to their closet, accept and acknowledge what had gone on in there, learn from it, be even more grateful for their existence and quality of life now and shut the door again. Yet she seemed to be the only one not only showing off her closet to the world but also using it as an excuse to constantly fail.

She wasn't good at leading because of her past, she wasn't good at communicating because of her past, she was aggressive because of her past, people don't like her because of her past, she was 37 and quite clearly had the maturity of a 17-year-old because she hadn't bitten the bullet and dealt with her past. You can't save everyone. But for Christ's sake, don't invite everyone you come into contact with to your own pity party and hand out your life story in the bloody party bags, especially in a process like this. You don't wake up one day with the shits and blame it on a dodgy curry you had ten years ago. Get a grip and understand whatever it is you have experienced has finished now and it is entirely your fault AND your responsibility if you continue to let it affect you.

As you can well imagine, we were halfway up the leisurely walk through the hills and our team were falling drastically behind. Recruit 20 had already abandoned the task of carrying her own Bergen (probably because of her past) dumping it on one of her team to carry and was doing a pretty shoddy job of organising, leading and even communicating with the people around her. I didn't feel I had much choice other than to intervene, otherwise, I feared we would be simultaneously thrown off the mountain one by one by the DS for being such an unmitigated shit-show. I stomped to the front of the pack (my Bergen still firmly on my back, may I add) and told everyone to put the log down. I then commanded my team.

"WE ARE GOING TO WORK IN 10-SECOND INTERVALS! WORK FOR 10 SECONDS THEN REST! I'LL COUNT AND GUIDE YOUR PATH."

I gave clear, concise instructions and I think people needed that. This task, yet again, was more about sheer willpower to get to the top rather than physicality. There was no way we were going to reach the other team by that point but I still wanted to maintain some pride by finishing before sunset. The relentless throbbing in my lower back, stomach and shoulders from lugging the dead weight of the Bergen and the log was thankfully masking the burn in my lungs the higher up the mountain we got. But my team were all suffering as well. As a leader, you have to be a pillar of positivity and composure irrespective of your personal condition. If I started to moan about the agony of getting through this task, that would start to infect the morale of my team like a rapid toxin, slowly draining the life out of all of them. You have to earn respect as a leader; you are not entitled to it. Recruit 20 continued with her pitiful,

"Well done, stay strong, keep moving..."

Which was an improvement on the last 2 hours but again, know your team members. These were some of the most driven, motivated people in the country. They didn't need positive feedback to enhance their performance, they needed stringent direction to get the task completed as efficiently as possible. Needless to say, 20 and I had some choice words throughout the hike and when eventually reaching the top, the DS quite rightly told us how utterly pathetic we were and ordered us to nominate the weakest members of the team. I took no satisfaction from the whole team nominating 20. I didn't want her to fail, I wanted her to get her head out of her arse, take responsibility and live a better existence than the one she was forcing herself to live out at the moment. But, unfortunately, her being the weakest was, of course, everyone else's fault and she missed yet another learning opportunity.

It was like a perfectly oiled TV machine that the next task following the log-carry happened to be the recruit boxing, which the show is quite well known for. The producers didn't even need to edit this section to create a bit of tension for the gripped audience at home. There was already enough hostility between recruit 20 and myself that, had it not been for the boxing task, she'd have probably laid one on me in my sleep anyway. I personally cannot remember a time in television history where a man and a woman were pitted against one another, toe to toe in a dingy, concrete boxing ring. This was revolutionary. Never mind women's rights. Never mind equal pay. This was the most impartial show of gender equality we'd ever seen. Of course, it doesn't matter what's between your legs in a fucking war. If you were the enemy you were going to get hurt; boobs, balls or whatever, it was irrelevant. This historical piece of television was a tiny piece of reality to the many ignorant out there and a genuine salute to all soldiers who serve us.

I was so desperate to fight a bloke. I thrived off the quiet appreciation associated with being female and choosing a male opponent in a toe to toe fistfight. Christ, I'd carved a life out of chasing brutal, typically male-dominated pursuits to ultimately prove my worth, so why stop now? Ok, we were unnecessarily padded out with head guards, gloves and a mouth guard but I'd have 100% taken a bloody nose or total unconsciousness if I had to, to ensure I gained the recognition of being brave enough to purposefully choose an opponent biologically stronger and more powerful than me. I wasn't scared by the oncoming prospect of a bruising uppercut or a thumping black eye; I thrived off the respect I would gain for choosing to put myself in inevitable danger and still fighting as hard as I bloody could throughout it. But obviously, teardrop had other ideas.

Due to her boxing background (apparently competing at a high level in the sport), when the DS asked for a volunteer, her hand went up quicker than a nursery child desperate for a piss. Obviously, she was going to pick me to fight against. The gargantuan chip on her shoulder was increasing in size by the minute and she felt she had a point to prove. In her eyes, I had embarrassed her in the log-carry by surpassing her intellectually, politically, verbally and as a leader. Therefore, she had to settle the score with her fists. This wasn't the honourable fight I had pictured. This wasn't the David and Goliath battle I wanted. This was her attempting to settle the score the only way she knew how, through violence and fighting. I had no choice but to participate and the deceptive selectivity of television editing didn't allow viewers to hear the part where we were directly instructed to administer no headshots. I'm not a violent person in the slightest, but we were being instructed to fight, so I was going to fucking fight. My initial plan was to land one right on her snout to give me a head start. That plan was scrapped immediately by the, in my opinion, rather unnecessary pre-fight instruction and I just decided to attack with every single reserve of energy I had.

I managed to land a good few blows on her torso as I came steaming out of the blocks. I found aggression I didn't even realise I had and hit and hit any area of her body I could. Needless to say, she did exactly the same to me and I winced as a few powerful strikes hit my ribs. The pain was greater than I expected in certain areas of my stomach, but I had no idea what was happening to my insides at that point. Undeterred, I carried on punching like a 1980's Rocky, throwing the most technically incorrect blows you've ever seen, until number 20 eventually delivered a blow that sent me to the floor and the fight was declared finished. So, in her narrow-minded and tragically uneducated brain, that was now us equalled out. In her eyes, a 5-minute clumsy scrap was enough to match the brave show of leadership and selfless team dedication I had displayed earlier in the day. But I congratulated her for her victory and allowed her to carry on her unfortunately unhappy existence. I quietly nursed my wounds and focused on whatever the next round of frivolity would be.

They left us alone after the boxing. Every other night would be interrupted in the early hours by a 'beasting' or a nice cold-water shower, but other than the obligatory hour on the watch post, we had an undisturbed sleep. I couldn't deny the pain in my stomach that seemed to be worsening daily. It definitely wasn't the time of the month and arguably we'd been eating some questionable meats over the course of the last few days, but even this felt worse than a dodgy mountain ferret salad. I continued to put it down to the altitude, overexertion and a few cracks in the ribs from my first amateur boxing experience and carried on.

We were adorned in snowshoes once more as we entered the early hours of day 6 of the entire process. Unbeknown to us, the plan was to trek us up to the base of the snowy Andes mountains once more and build ourselves a shelter. Once the shelter was built, we were due to have a little sleepover in there where we could do hair, nails and face masks and talk ex-boyfriends and diet pills. This was where the set-up of the programme was very clever; yet again, we were being thrown into the complete unknown. If someone had mentioned we would essentially be building a glorified snow castle, in freezing temperatures, with no more than a couple of shovels and our bare hands, then sleeping in the damn thing, we maybe wouldn't have clambered up the mountain so enthusiastically. But we did, because we were a gutsy group of individuals, relentlessly persevering through this process, whatever it may throw at us.

The evening was drawing in as we began to construct our snow shelters. I was allocated as leader again for this task and the DS were more than complimentary of my ability;

"Whatever you do, don't fuck this up, number 5."

I couldn't work out whether the sudden shiver down my spine was the bitter cold, the kind message I'd just received inconceivably close to my ear lobe, or the psychological pressure building yet again through the thought of undertaking quite an intimidating task none of us had ever come close to doing before. The Bergens acted as the base of the snow shelter. We had to walk out a clearing in the snow for the military rucksacks to be placed in, before piling copious amounts of snow on top. This would then create a dome around the Bergens, and, upon removal of them from the pile of snow, a hollow would be created within the shelter for us to all cosily bed down for the night. The incredible expanse that we were surrounded by could have easily made for the best snowball fight in the world. We were like little dots on a huge A3 sheet of paper, pure white blanket snow for miles and miles, so there certainly wasn't the worry we would run out of supplies to build our temporary home.

Oh, and the bitter cold? That soon disappeared too as sweat started to trickle off my nose. The labour-intensive task of shovelling and piling snow, on top of snow, on top of snow was enough to create a funnel of steam, emanating from our sweaty heads like a freshly boiled kettle.

Once the dome was fully complete, we then had the unenviable task of diving back into it and hauling the Bergens back out. We took it in turns to burrow away at the snow like little field mice searching for their next scrap of food. Energy was literally dripping out of us with each and every desperate claw at the snow. I was ardently willing my team on with our incessant task, all whilst continually feeling pretty rank. That dodgy ferret salad and rice I mentioned previously must have passed through my system by then, but the way I was feeling, apparently it hadn't. We were in near darkness by the time our snow shelter was complete and I was incredibly proud of the team effort to complete it. Don't get me wrong, it was no 5-star boutique room with a swan-shaped hand towel and complimentary pillow chocolates. But, if the proverbial brown stuff were to hit the oscillating cooling device, it would have sheltered us from the elements. Basically, we would have been safe had the shit hit the fan. I was more than ready to bed down with a nice canteen of ice-cold water, but the weather conditions took a considerable turn for the worse. Before I could even finish my bedtime story or pop my slippers on, the head torches were out and the snowshoes were donned to make our way back to the awaiting vehicles, as there was a storm coming. It was an extraordinary experience trekking through pure white snow whilst also surrounded by a magnificent sheet of black above us. The temperature seemed to have dropped even more as the tracks we had created on the journey up the mountain had frozen over and delicately crunched underfoot. We trekked in silence through the darkness, still maintaining quite the pace to outrun the ominous storm and finally, the military vehicles were in sight again. I was so glad to be rid of the snowshoes which were basically oversized plastic flip flops with spikes in the bottom that skidded off your feet every 5 steps. I was half expecting yet another curveball and the vehicles to drive off infront of our despairing faces leaving us all to lunge back to the accommodation or something ridiculous. Gratefully, I was wrong as we piled into the back of the green canvas of the trucks once more. I must have fallen asleep pretty much as soon as we set off, my exhausted, frozen, broken body desperate for a rest.

We were hitting midnight by the time we returned to the accommodation to a welcoming warm meal of plain chicken and rice. I felt like I could barely stomach my own oxygen by that point but knew I needed to try and get some food inside me. It took about 5 minutes to chew and digest a grain of rice and a mouthful of chicken. There was no point me trying to get to sleep as it was my shift on the observation post between 2am and 3am. I sat with my fellow recruit watching the rain piss all over camp for 60 tiresome minutes before returning to my sodden sleeping bag that had succumbed to the crack in the window and was now only 70% dry. The unfortunate 30% that had been exposed to the rain was, of course, where my head should have lain. The unknown creature that seemed to be eating my insides wasn't ready for bed either. I went to the large trunk at the entrance of the accommodation to fish out some paracetamol, hoping it would take the edge off the most unimaginable pain in the top of my stomach. I was fiercely battling on my camp bed to try and get into a comfortable position and at least get a few minutes of rest. This was turning into much more than just a dull ache; my diaphragm felt like it was attacking me with every inhalation I made. If anything, I was grateful when the wooden door nearly came off its hinges as the DS came bursting through the door at 5am, demanding we get on the parade square, just to try and have something to take my mind off the pain I was in and the 13 minutes of sleep that I'd had.

Within minutes, we were crawling round the puddle-filled parade square scattered with broken rocks and glass. I was desperately dragging myself along, momentarily checking that one of the broken shards of rock hadn't penetrated my stomach and I was gushing claret all over the place. That's certainly what felt like was happening to my insides. The directing staff were hounding me second by second as I was so obviously behind the pace. I was struggling to put one foot in front of the other let alone think about carrying another human being on my shoulders. I was not giving up. I didn't care how much I was suffering; I refused to give up during the beasting as it would appear I couldn't cope with the demands of physical exertion. It was enough of a knock on my pride that my body appeared to be capitulating in front of me. I was not giving up for anything or anyone. After a solid hour of uninterrupted agony, the beasting was over and I knew then that I couldn't continue. There was something seriously wrong. I found the energy to return to the accommodation with my fellow recruits only to secretly sneak out again, preparing to reluctantly hand in my numbered armband and voluntarily withdraw. The DS came out to meet me as I stood dejected and beaten in front of him.

"What's going on, number 5?" Directing Staff Matthew 'Ollie' Ollerton had come to meet me at the communication point.

"I'm done, staff, physically and psychologically I'm done."

I quietly muttered my words withholding my overwhelming emotion.

"Well, you've done yourself proud, number 5, remember that."

I was not expecting this genuine, complimentary response which was paired with a momentary embrace and pat on the back. I don't do well with compliments and this entirely positive response to my performance from such an experience soldier did nothing for the emotional state I was already in. It was over; the dream I'd had of completing one of the most brutal military selection courses in the worldwas not achieved. I was broken. Completely broken. In so many more ways than one.

Chapter 8.

Recovery Version 2.0

There should have been a prominent feeling of disappointment overpowering every part of my mind. I should have been totally frustrated, dejected, and heartbroken that my SAS experience was over well before its time. But any feeling of disappointment I may have experienced was just masked by indescribable pain that had torn its way through the whole of my torso. My exit interview - a 20-minute discussion where the show's psychologist gently ascertains whether you are leaving the process with any long-term psychological issues - had to be cut short; which turned out to be a long-term problem in itself. Just as I was about to elaborate on the mental torment of having to prematurely leave an incredibly important life experience because of an uncontrollable, extremely painful, external variable, I vomited, nearly to the brim of a bag for life, after which I just pleaded for somewhere dry and warm to lie down. So, to that end, we never really established whether I was leaving the show with any long-term psychological issues at all. The course doctor led me into a cargo container that had been adapted for the camera crew with a camp bed and table. It was warm, dry and quiet and held the guarantee of no unwanted interruptions to perform handstands in freezing water or to throw oneself off a cliff face. I nestled down into the sleeping bag as far as I could in the hope that more than 20 minutes' sleep would solve what on earth was happening to my insides. I must have fallen asleep instantly through sheer exhaustion because it felt like seconds before I was awoken again to be assessed.

"How are you feeling, Laura?"

I tend to play down how much pain I'm in usually, as a matter of pride, but I couldn't hide away from whatever was happening this time.

"Horrendous, mate, I'm in a lot of pain."

He must have literally held his hand on my stomach, a feather would have put more pressure on, and even that slight touch invited an agonising scream. With no word of warning and no explanation, he stormed outside, barking orders to the group of crew members standing around the entrance to the container, like they were queuing for a tourist attraction. I couldn't make out what he was saying but the fast-paced and aggressive enunciation of his words was enough for me to become even more concerned. What the hell was going on? Emily, one of the lovely assistant producers, the maternal matriarch of the production crew, came into the cabin with a plate of bourbon biscuits and a banana. That was the most heavenly sight I'd seen in 7 days. I was ready to devour all 8 of them before Sundeep then burst back into the container,

"LAURA, DO NOT EAT THOSE BISCUITS!!'

It is a very brave man that orders me not to eat bourbons at the best of times, never mind in the dire straits of that portable cabin. He was lucky it wasn't a Jammy Dodger. No man woman or child would have stopped a JD going down in there. Thankfully, I lowered the biscuit (that was desperately close to my lips) just in time after his command and looked to him for what needed to be a bloody good reason not to eat my bourbon.

"I believe you have got quite a severe case of appendicitis. We need to get you to a hospital as soon as possible."

Unbelievably, my first thought was,

"Thank God for that; it is something really serious. I'm not going to look like a complete pansy now."

My second thought was,

"A hospital? It would be quicker if I inserted a coat hanger up my rear end and pulled it out myself. We are miles and miles and miles away from any sort of civilisation out here. It would take hours to get to hospital."

Finally, in my warped order of priority, I then came to the realisation,

"Hang on, don't people die from appendicitis?"

Yes. Yes, they do. And considering I'd been battling with mine for most of the week, we were getting into pretty dangerous territory by then. The other crew doctors came in straight away to start administering morphine, which was the best thing to enter my body in well over a week. I was blissfully unaware that all and sundry were frantically calling the majority of the Chilean authorities in an attempt to get a helicopter to come out to our location. The crew got in contact with both the Chilean Police and the Chilean Military who both flatly refused to send a helicopter out because of the inclement weather conditions. I was walking to hospital at this rate. As much as the crew attempted to keep me calm, I could sense the trepidation in the atmosphere as well as amongst the staff, and actually started to have my own concerns about my welfare. I tried to control my fear but the combination of sleep deprivation and being surrounded by near-strangers in my time of need, I started to catastrophise the whole situation. Unlike the trustworthy harness that held me tightly over the rock face, I wasn't confident over my safety in that situation. I didn't have any control over the danger I was in now. I had no metaphorical harness to keep me safe. My appendix was on the verge of bursting, with my nearest friends and family a 14-hour flight away on the other side of the world. I was still in one of the most remote areas of Chile you could wish for, with not much hope of getting an emergency helicopter ride any time soon. But at least we had bourbons. Oh, wait, I wasn't allowed them either because of the apparently imminent surgery. There was nothing at all imminent about the surgery if you asked me, no fucker wanted to send out a chopper in these conditions. And who could blame them? Christ, if the military refused, where was our next port of call?

The course doctor offered to phone my next of kin to explain what was going on. I gallantly refused, not wanting my partner, Amanda, to worry. Just imagine it. You know full well your partner of, at the time, 5 years is participating in a ruthless course of military-type training halfway across the world and you haven't had any direct or indirect contact with them since they landed in the country. Believe it or not, updating your Facebook status to 'Fuck me, I'm knackered' with a mountain-top selfie is not part of Special Forces selection training. Your thoughts are already completely preoccupied with what on earth is happening to them on a daily basis and you also know full well you won't hear a peep out of them until they complete the course, get kicked off the course, voluntarily withdraw from the course or something else more serious. My hay-fever started to get bad as soon as I heard her voice.

"Hi Amanda, this is the SAS course doctor speaking. I have Laura here with me."

"Ok, is everything ok? Has she handed her number in?"

Amanda knew me. She knew I would not give up my number for anything or anyone. I wanted to complete that course or (quite literally) die trying. Well, I hadn't completed it; I'd nearly done the other option.

"No, unfortunately not; she has handed her number in but is a little bit unwell at the moment and we are in the process of airlifting her to hospital for emergency surgery."

I can't begin to understand what that conversation was like for Amanda. The person you love most in the world is about to undergo life-saving surgery, you haven't spoken for 7 days, but you are 2 flights and 14 hours away and there is absolutely nothing you can do to help. I tried to swallow the lump in my throat to talk to her,

"Hi, baby. I had to hand my number in. I'm so sorry, I was just in too much pain."

Straight away, my priority was to try and justify the fact I hadn't completed what I set out to. Despite my physical condition, I was already ensuring the outside world knew I didn't just give up, I was really quite ill. My physical and psychological resilience are two of the very few personal qualities I take pride in and to have either of them questioned, doubted or criticised in any way was verging on unbearable for me. Obviously, Amanda was far less concerned with my progression throughout the course and more with my actual health. I could hear her voice trembling as I promised to call her when we got to the hospital and told her, rather pointlessly, not to worry.

Every conceivable thought entered my brain in the time it was taking to organise my trip to somewhere, anywhere that wasn't where we were. It would be quite a cool way to die.. I'd be a hero when people found out... That has never happened before... I'd be honoured... I'd come up on the screen of deceased people at the television awards with the violinist playing in the background... Shit. What about Amanda? How will they get my body back? Am I insured? Will they show me dying on the TV? Will I get a pay-out? Will they pay for my funeral?

"SHUT UP, LAURA!"

You are not dead yet. Somehow, I still don't know how, a private hospital in Santiago, Clínica Alemana de Santiago, to be precise, agreed to send out their helicopter if we were able to get to a village school field around 20 miles from where we were. I would love to be able to tell you how much this was costing the Channel, but truth be told, I don't know. I'd like to think the budget for series 4 tripled because of my spontaneous excursion. Little did I know that my helicopter holiday 9 years previously on the A14, was going to be only my first airbornelife-saving journey. Apparently, I would be enjoying a second, just this time I knew exactly what was going on around me, was completely conscious and I was 14 hours over the other side of the world, not a quick hour down the road. I think I'd take being unconscious with severe concussion any day over being acutely aware of just how much danger you are in.

The only trouble we then had was that the closest thing we had resembling an ambulance to get me to said school field, were those blasted military trucks we had been piling in and out of all week. What we were functioning on out there was beyond basic, but surely, we could find some transportation that was mildly more comfortable than a canvas-covered wagon with makeshift benches for stretchers? My racing mind was temporarily pacified by the spare Range Rover that came to the rescue in this completely ridiculous saga. Why I thought the Range Rover would be more comfortable I don't know. It didn't smell of mouldy canvas so that was enough of an improvement to trust it and get hauled into the back. The pathway that led to the old miner's camp we stayed in - hang on, pathway makes it sound like a lovely cycle route through a quiet suburb that you cheerfully pedal down on a Sunday afternoon - the jagged, rocky, unbalanced track that led us to camp was like an adolescent complexion. It was dotted with countless divots and potholes for the driver to meander around, whilst also attempting to keep straight so as not to drive off the side of the mountain. It was like driving through a huge game of 'Whack a Mole.' Every single slight bump or alteration in gradient we came across shot through my entire body. Lying completely still was agony enough without having to cope with this roller coaster ride as well.

The combination of those few hours instantaneously gave me an appreciation of our society, where we live and how simple it is for us to reach medical care in an emergency. I'd never before had to worry about the quality of the roads that led to medical care. I know the

A14 can be a bloody nightmare on a Friday afternoon, but I'd take that over the Chilean cross-country driving experience any day. After a few choice words between me and Alan the appendix, we were finally entering territory that resembled civilisation. I could see a black helicopter waiting for me, parked up in grass surroundings. Waiting for me?? This whole debacle was unquestionably life-threatening, far too close for comfort at times. But yet again, my slightly distorted perception of the world took over and I found this unmitigated disaster quite exciting. A helicopter, from a private hospital in the centre of Chile, has flown out in treacherous weather conditions to take me to hospital for emergency surgery, because I contracted appendicitis, halfway up The Andes Mountains, building snow shelters, whilst participating in a replication of one of the most brutal military selection processes in the world. Oh, and it is all due to be shown on national television too. Just re-read that sentence. If that is not an unforgettable life experience, I don't know what is.

Whilst I was lying in increasing discomfort planning these very pages in my mind, everyone else was frantically loading me on board to get to the hospital. I suppose I should have been grateful in some way; not many people get to experience one life-saving helicopter journey, never mind two. The morphine began freely flowing around my body so at least I had some relief and an actual recollection of this second helicopter journey. So, I did all I could do, stare horizontally out of the window and take in some more breath-taking views. On arrival at the hospital, I was wheeled off for an MRI scan to confirm what we already knew. It was confirmed I had appendicitis and needed to be prepared for surgery as soon as possible. I was completely overcome with the most surreal feeling of vulnerability. Whenever you head in for surgery of any kind, there is a slight feeling of trepidation and unease. It is only human to be slightly apprehensive of these strangers cutting you open and playing 'hook a duck' with your insides. But this was different. I was so alone. I couldn't understand anything that was being said to me and it takes me years to build trust with anyone, let alone these very well-intentioned strangers who were trying to undress me. I mean, rather them than me at that point when you consider I hadn't seen a shower for the best part of 7 days. These people were all doing their very best to help me and I couldn't be anything but grateful, but all I craved was a familiar face. I needed someone to wrap their arms around me and tell me that this entirely unbelievable experience would actually end up being ok; someone to reiterate to me a quote that I live by,

"Everything will be ok in the end; if it is not ok, it is not the end."

But it certainly wasn't the end just yet. Thankfully, one of the show's runners, Mercedes, was fluent in Spanish but even she was a good couple of hours away. I was being handed clipboards to sign to ensure I consented to the surgery I was undertaking. For all I knew, I was agreeing for them to take out a bloody lung. The anaesthetist was very talented and her bi-lingual

218

ability was so reassuring. I'd always wanted to learn a second language and if this little outing wasn't motivation enough to do so, I don't know what would be. There may as well have been hieroglyphics on the walls of the pristinely clean hospital corridors that we were travelling down, but I assumed they knew where they were going. I still couldn't help but feel unsafe, despite the fact I was now in a squeaky-clean private hospital as opposed to the derelict miner's camp I'd been plucked from just hours previously. I soon drifted off so that Alan the appendix could be safely removed before he could burst and make this shit storm any worse than it already was.

The care I received in the hospital was second to none. I looked forward to the grammatically incorrect messages that were written, without fail, on my room's whiteboard every morning,

"Don't worries, be smile." Or "Be happy, you would be fine."

I completely admired the nurses' attempt to write a morale-boosting message, not in their first language, for my benefit alone, so, I wasn't going to be correcting any glaring errors this time. However, having your appendix removed only allows for a very limited post-operation diet. Anything full of fat, full of flavour or fried (all of the good stuff basically) was completely out of bounds. I was on a solid diet of chicken, rice and dry crackers for a week. When you have already just experienced a week of rather ambiguous meals, all I wanted to do was devour a great big cheese toasty or great big dirty burger, but that would have to continue to be put on hold.

I had to wait a few days before I was allowed to fly home and we were put up in a beautiful little Chilean farmhouse surrounded by more flowing greenery and roaming goats. Most other recruits would leave the process, grab a much-needed shower, spend a night at the farm and be on the flight home the next morning. I had to watch them all come and go whilst I waited to be allowed to fly, explaining to each and everyone the situation and watching their jaws drop to the floor when they realised it wasn't just a sickness bug. Every other recruit left the process understandably shattered but fulfilled. They had personally reached their breaking point or had been instructed by the Directing Staff they were not capable enough to continue. Either way, they had some form of closure on their experience. They had gone as far as they were able to. Physically, I had to be withdrawn because there was a high chance I'd have died if I hadn't. Something happened completely beyond my control which ended my experience for me. But I wasn't done; psychologically I had so much more to give, and even 48 hours after surgery it was niggling away at me; I'd failed. I'd not achieved what I wanted to. Had I not been capable enough on day 1 and I'd been culled, I could have accepted that. Had I pushed and pushed and pushed and psychologically couldn't stand another minute, I could have accepted that. But to have a completely unexpected and external variable pop along and infiltrate my body, putting a premature end to one of

220

the most important experiences of my life, at the time, I could not accept that. I berated myself if I was 2 seconds over my 5k PB time, let alone something on the scale that SAS was. At a time when all I needed to do was be kind to myself, to take pride in the huge accomplishment even getting picked for the show was, as well as being labelled a capable leader whilst on it and to just take a moment to congratulate myself – all I was doing was planning what to do to next to compensate for what I deemed to be a failure. My mindset was not helped in the slightest when the show came to air on national television in January 2019 at the prime slot of 9pm on a Sunday night.

To my great satisfaction, I was actually depicted quite well in the early episodes of the show. I had positive exposure and some of my leadership and tenacity was displayed, which I was appreciative of. Considering others get a quick snapshot in the opening credits and that's their lot, I was content with the acknowledgement I received. As much as I, amongst many others, genuinely didn't participate for the 5 minutes of fame, the whole adventure taught me that the television industry is brutal and that the public are generally naive to television tricks of the trade. Editors can manipulate any footage they want to ensure it portrays the dramatic story they have created, as opposed to the factual truth. Any altercation, minor controversy or slight area of contention can be exploited to leave some poor unsuspecting individual as public enemy number one. But we knew exactly what we were signing up for and that is, unfortunately, what brings in the viewing figures. We are sadistic as a nation. We don't want to see achievement and co-operation. We are gripped by suffering, confrontation and bare-faced failure. I was nothing short of mortified upon hearing the planned portrayal of my exit.

We received phone calls from the producers the previous day before the show was aired, to inform us of our involvement in the next episode. I was informed, quite abruptly, that I would be shown handing my number in after the beasting, but there was to be no inclusion of the glaringly obvious reason behind it. There would not be so much as a 5-second voice over to explain I was airlifted to hospital for life-saving surgery. Not once were they prepared to allude to the fact I withdrew because I was in a life-threatening situation, not because I just couldn't be arsed anymore. I was being convinced over the phone call that my exit was honourable, dignified and noble. How could I remain dignified when my exit was being depicted untruthfully? I might have extracted some self-respect from the episode had the real reason behind my withdrawal been publicised, but it wasn't. It was remarkably obvious from the way the show was edited, that I appeared to just give up. But I didn't. To say this destroyed me psychologically was the understatement of the century. I watched the episode behind clenched hands, partially blocking my vision, just waiting for the onslaught of confused messages from excited friends following my journey. That's the other caveat around television appearances; you legally can't tell anyone (other than your family) what the hell happened. So, the inevitable invasion of text messages commenced, literally minutes after the episode was aired.

"MATE! You were doing so well! Can't believe you handed your number in!"

"You had so much more to give!"

"I thought you were going to go all the way!"

"What happened? It's so not like you to give up!"

I rudely ignored the majority of them because I couldn't contemplate explaining this monumental kick in the teeth on a repetitive basis. So, I killed numerous birds with one stone and put a carefully constructed, delicately worded, photograph-proofed social media post out explaining the real reasons behind my departure. On any normal day, when I'm documenting the fine details of my avocado on toast breakfast on Facebook or the 'Gram', I'm lucky if I get 30 likes; this thing got nearly 25,000. 25,000 people knew the truth behind what had happened and this, sadly, gave me some reassurance. I most certainly shouldn't have needed any validation from complete strangers to settle my despondency. I shouldn't have needed to project my story all over a wide-reaching platform to know that what I achieved was worthwhile and I deserved a bit of recognition for what I'd endured.

Had I got my chance again, I'd sit on what really happened, entirely content that I and those close to me knew exactly what happened and that's all that is important. There is no need for the external endorsement of others to solidify your achievement with any physical or psychological success. Does a bright blue thumbs-up from a complete stranger enhance what you have achieved in any way? I don't think so. SAS: Who Dares Wins was a huge insight and learning curve for me to ensure you consistently congratulate yourself for every single small victory, irrespective of whether it is being plastered all over national television or not. You need to be secure enough in yourself to be able to acknowledge surmounting even the smallest of hurdles. The success of an accomplishment does, by no means whatsoever, correlate with the number of people who know about it. Go and achieve something extraordinary because you will be the one to remember and recite it 50 years from now, not because the window cleaner will know about it when you see him at the weekend. Go and push the boundaries because you want to, not because you'll receive plaudits on a screen. Over-achieve because it is what you are personally determined to do, not because the recognition is what drives you. Be ok with people not knowing your side of the story. You have nothing to prove to anyone.

Chapter 9.
Marathon 6-10

After day 5, it was like I had got to the top of the gargantuan mountain I was climbing and all we had to do now was navigate our way down. At that point, I had gained a lot of unexpected confidence in the fact I'd covered 131 miles in 5 days relatively unscathed and there was no reason why I couldn't do that again. Amanda and I were out of the door by 6:30am on day 6 to hit the road to Brighton, a location that had to be included in the list of 10, not just because of its seaside charm, colourful uniqueness, gorgeous surroundings and effervescent community but also because it was the location where I ran my first ever marathon. My tummy flipped with excitement as we drove into Brighton and heard the first squawk of a seagull and caught our first glimpse of the beautiful coastline. We bloody loved this place and as I started up yet again on my (at that stage) very slow and steady 11-minute per mile marathon pace, the sea air filled my lungs, I saw my first ice cream stall and I was so content. I'd trained for the long slow miles. I knew that by the second half of the week, my usual 8 minutes 30 per mile pace would be completely unrealistic. I had trained long and slow and that was what my body had become accustomed to. Any runner knows that running slower than your normal pace is probably harder than running faster than your normal pace. But I had slowed my pace because that was exactly what this challenge demanded. It was the most sensible option to achieve the longevity and consistency needed every day. Brighton represented everything running was for me; the freedom, the breath-taking views, the feeling of being complete and the knowledge you are sharing your favourite thing in the world with your favourite people in the world, all so valiantly behind you.

Mand and I thought it was going to be a quiet little marathon, just the two of us trickling along the seafront, ticking off the miles. But the incredible effort shown by my closest friends was once again displayed in all its glory as four of my closest friends, Annalise, Lee, Naomi and Nadine surprised us along Brighton Sea Front. I'm not sure why I was surprised any more. The indisputable commitment, allegiance and downright dedication my friends were showing towards my endeavours was never in doubt throughout the whole ten days. Those people travelled halfway across the country to make sure their slightly obsessed mate was kept company at the seaside as they ran and cycled with me near enough the whole way. The sun shone on us all day long as we ran up and down Brighton seafront and alongside the striking white cliffs leading out to Rottingdean. The sun just glistened and sparkled off the English Channel and lit up our already radiant faces. We were like a little dream team roaming in and out of the piles of pebbles and sand left by the rising tide. Brighton seafront periodically had outdoor showers for the sun-kissed beach dwellers to rinse off at the end of a busy day building sandcastles and jumping the waves. I was so grateful of a fully clothed cold shower every few miles and I happily came out drenched to the core and squelching along the promenade in search of the next refreshing convenience.

We picked up a lime-flavoured Callipo at around mile 16 and I swear to God it was the best thing I had ever tasted. I had quickly mastered the quite particular skill of eating whilst running over the last few days but that limey iced block barely even touched the sides. Day 6 was nothing short of perfection and the miles just seemed to fly by. We'd set up the finish line just outside the iconic I-360 British Airways tourist attraction so we only had 4 miles to complete along the older part of Brighton seafront to reach 26.2. The only problem was we had to get down a rather substantial flight of stairs to finish off the last few miles of marathon number 6. I approached the stairs with sturdy confidence, wrongly thinking I'd safely descend them with my 22-mile warm-up to prepare me. I stepped down and completely changed the movement pattern my right knee had become accustomed too over the last 4 hours and nearly collapsed there and then in a very undignified heap. I could not walk down the bloody stairs. I gripped on to the handrail like a petrified rock climber and slowly tried to gain some control over my legs. This whole thing was actually completely hilarious to any bemused onlooker.

But, a monumental descent down a set of concrete stairs was exactly what I did not need with still 4 more marathons to run. Thankfully, Mand came to save the day yet again as she grabbed my arm and escorted me down the stairs like an inpatient in a geriatric ward and we cracked on with the nice flat last 4 miles. I felt invincible at Brighton. The combination of it being my absolute favourite place in the world, along with some fantastically unexpected company, the orgasmic Callipo and just pacing the whole run really well contributed to such a memorable day. Of course, we crossed the finish line with a huge smile and had a very welcome sea ice bath, sat in the backdrop of the eerie but strangely beautiful remains of the burnt-out old pier. Brighton has to be a contender for the best day of 10-10-10 but there were 9 others that were pretty special as well. Brighton felt like the day, and all runners have them, where I could have run forever. It is difficult to top that feeling.

Coronavirus hadn't allowed us to book a hotel for the night, so in 24 hours, we drove 2 and a half hours to Brighton, did a marathon, grabbed some fish and chips, sat and basked in yet another brilliant achievement and then drove what we thought would be the 2 and a half hours home. That 2 and a half hours soon turned into a 4-hour trek to get home when we were ground to a halt in the stickiest of traffic jams on the M11. I would have omitted the rather boring journey home, however, it provided huge hilarity for everyone involved when I desperately needed a wee about an hour into the aforementioned traffic jam. Thankfully, we had a car full of empty water bottles and I had to choose very carefully the correct size rim on the particular water bottle in order to prevent unwanted spillages. My very fatigued legs had to somehow lift me very tactically out of my plush leather car seat, just high enough in order to aim with precise accuracy into my favourite Lucozade bottle. The perfect circumference of the top of the bottle provided just enough room to decant a day's worth of hydration into it and we quietly poured it out of the window in stationary traffic and no one was any the wiser. The bottle was then given a quick wipe over and used to slurp out of the next day. I was going to be really adventurous and see if I could recycle the warm, brown liquid I decanted into it on marathon 7 and try to pass it off as some sort of complex sports apple juice used for top-notch hydration, but I decided what came out of a tap as opposed to my insides might be slightly safer.

It was a real learning curve attempting to get on top of the nutrition and hydration required for such an endurance event and, 7 days in, I was just about working it out. Living off glucose-saturated energy drinks and artificial fried-egg-shaped sugar treats for the first 2 marathons left my insides nothing more than a messy, gurgling whirlpool with no real substance to survive off. The daily routine would consist of a substantial breakfast (1 hour pre-run) of porridge, bacon butties, dippy eggs or multiple rounds of wholemeal toast with lashings of butter and marmite. Then, during each run, I'd learned to have a quick pit stop at miles 10, 16 and sometimes 22 in order to eat actual food – not glucose-infused substances that take years to decay (in both your stomach and the outside world). I'd be grabbing bananas, flapjacks and protein bars on the go, consistently perfecting my eating, sweating and breathing technique. For one solitary marathon, you would never dream of having an on-the-go picnic to get you round, but for 10 of the buggers back to back, I'm surprised I wasn't employing a Deliveroo moped to follow me around every day. The sacrifice I had to face was that for 10 days straight I'd be eating a good breakfast, having a banana for lunch and then trying to force down some dinner after around 8 hours without a proper meal, all whilst burning around 5,000 calories per day. It was like an extreme diet plan you'd find on a dodgy foreign website and the weight was falling off me. I couldn't put enough back in for what I was burning off. On the rare occasion when I did feel a pang of hunger, it resembled the sort of craving you get mid-morning after a mammoth night on the lash. I wanted chips, burgers, bacon - anything fried and with 4 tablespoons of salt in one mouthful. The fish and chips we devoured at Brighton were probably the most generous meal I'd eaten all week. So, I continued to apply the rather luxurious principle of eating exactly what I wanted, how much of it I wanted and when I wanted it. Trying to periodically consume spinach salads and vegan pomegranate bites was all very well-planned, but it just couldn't hit the spot like strategically consuming half a tube of salt and vinegar crisps at 7am, 11am and again at 8pm.

Day 7 provided hydration of a different but very welcome kind that we had been longing for since day 1- it finally rained. The gentle pitter-patter on my bedroom window was a wonderful wake-up call as I gently rolled out of bed to get ready to celebrate a week of running daily marathons. The route for day 7 was so simple, I was thankful to have no directional logistics to work out following our stupendous journey just hours previously. The guided bus route precisely 0.2 miles away from my front door was exactly 13.1 miles of long, flat and traffic-free tarmac that was a runner's paradise. All I had to do was run to one end and run back again and pick up some more brilliantly supportive runners en route. The guided bus meant I could continuously see for miles and miles and miles ahead of me, but psychologically, the mind-numbing simplicity of it made it very easy to tick away at the miles. However, I'm not entirely sure this would be the best seller I'd hoped for, if I try and fill the next 3 pages with enthralling stories and analysis of the 13-mile long tarmac track. I will squeeze the positives out of absolutely anything. I'd get a cup of crystal-clear water out of a dry sponge if I tried hard enough, but attempting to make the 26.2 miles along the guided bus route sound exciting is beyond even me. We ran the long tarmac path to one end and we ran back. It was a marathon and we still had some hardy, committed supporters en route and that was all that mattered. The sheer commitment of my friends, old and new, to come out in the rain to endure the straight, long, tarmac turmoil was yet more inspiration for me to kick back and carry on – for their sake as well as mine.

I think my support team manager, personal assistant and right-hand woman (for literally everything), Amanda, started to understandably feel the mental, physical and emotional fatigue by day 7. It was only on day 7 that I really started to see and appreciate how this was all affecting her as well. I couldn't help but feel horrifically guilty on that Wednesday afternoon, after we had paraded up and down the guided bus route for 5 hours in pissing rain; she got home, took off her soaking wet clothes and was asleep on the sofa by 3pm. I felt like I was slowly breaking her down just as much as I was myself, yet you didn't hear her complain once. Yes, I was running 26.2 miles every day but she was cycling alongside me too. If you've ever tried cycling, on a mountain bike, at the same pace as a woman running a marathon a day for 10 days across multiple different terrains, you'll know exactly what that does to your back, bum and brain. Cycling at a normal pace for that amount of time is uncomfortable, let alone slowing down enough to accompany this tortoise stuck in peanut butter. I had the pure adrenaline and achievement factor pulsing through me at the end of every marathon to keep me buzzing from day to day. She was achieving everything alongside me but I was the one receiving all the plaudits. She was cooking the meals, packing the car, driving the car, keeping up with the enquiries from friends and family, unpacking the car, washing clothes, buying supplies, remembering supplies, fixing punctures, rubbing my sore limbs and carefully tending to my often battered emotional state – her list was endless; so endless that it made my job of putting one foot in front of the other for a few hours a day seem easy. We maintained our delicious hangover food diet that evening with some bacon and egg butties, in some donated homemade rolls and hit the hay at about 8pm.

Day 8 soon came round and it began to feel, for the first time, like we were actually going to achieve this bold little thing I'd been dreaming about for months. We still had 78.6 miles to cover in 3 days and, whilst I had never allowed my own self-belief to dwindle, I was still intimidated back on days 1 and 2 by what I was taking on. We'd chipped away at that quite overwhelming mountain of miles day by day and arrived at a point where what we were doing didn't seem so far out of reach. It clearly started to become more serious to those following the challenge hiding in the shadows as well. I know I'm in danger of sounding like a broken record here, but the support for 10-10-10 from *most* was unwavering and unconditional from day 1. And that was day 1 of planning, organising and promoting months before even1 day of running. Months before we even started, people showed their commitment to what I was doing and I couldn't have been more grateful for that. But there is always, unfortunately, that small minority of people who think you might fail in your extreme endeavours or, tragically, want to see you fail. So, they don't bother openly showing their support (especially on such a vast platform as social media) in the early stages, for fear of looking ridiculous when the cause does inevitably crumble. We were far from crumbling and the increase in encouragement from those previously silent supporters in the final third of the 10 days was noticeable. I'll take positive support in any way, shape or form and show my gratitude for it. Although, the increasing amount of people that started crawling out of the woodwork, who had been completely non-existent in the pitfalls of having to postpone the challenge or in the darker fatigue, illness-ridden days at the beginning of the adventure, was obvious. I took from their slightly delayed support that they did actually want to attend the positivity party we had been having for 8 days, but were just a little bit late and turned up with a cheap bottle of wine. That was fine; anyone was more than welcome on our positivity parade which continued through Thetford on day 8. That gorgeous Friday morning, as we started to trundle on again around the stunning backdrop of Thetford Forest, the realisation we were getting close to the finish was upon us all.

Thetford was the first real multi-terrain route we had encountered along the way. Even though it conjured up some fantastic memories of childhood cross-country running and the stunning scenery we were running through took my breath away, the toll it took on my already vulnerable body was hard-hitting. Unlike any other day so far, I had to intensely concentrate on where I was placing my foot on every single step. The floor was like a less colourful version of the London underground map, except the Victoria and Northern lines were replaced with scattered brown tree roots, logs, branches and bushes protruding out of the ground. Our rural underground was providing very real potential for a twisted ankle around every corner. The meandering forest also took us up inclines and down declines and whilst the grin widened across my face like an excitable child at every opportunity to leg it down a hill, downhill running also became quite an uncomfortable sensation too. The Thetford route was made up of two 10.5-mile loops and one 5-mile loop so it was easy to manage food intake, and being the beautiful location that it was, my support crew for day 8 was just fantastic. A very good friend of mine, Aimee, brought her husband, James, to come and smash out a whole marathon by my side. James was a military man and was using the route as training for an upcoming course, so he carried a 20kg Bergen on his back for the first 20 miles. James acted as fantastic inspiration for me that day. I love it when other people push their comfort zones in the relentless pursuit to better themselves, and doing it whilst keeping me company too was even better. He soldiered on beside me that day without a word of complaint, despite being in considerable discomfort within the final few miles. And, from the foundations of being a relative stranger at the start of the day, through the shared appreciation of exercise, perseverance and endurance, we forged a firm friendship over 26.2 miles together. The finish of day 8 was just as awe-inspiring as the 7 that had preceded it. Another bespoke medal was placed around my neck and the team sense of achievement was thoroughly enjoyed and embraced by all. I literally couldn't stop smiling.

The mental and physical concentration required to conquer Thetford Forest, I think, had wiped everyone out that day and I started to feel the slight niggles in my knees and shins starting to get angrier and angrier. The battle to decide whether I was in pain or just discomfort continued as I desperately tried to convince myself it was just discomfort. Foot placement concentration levels needed to be very much on point for day 9 as well. Marathon 9 consisted of a 3-lap route around another multi-terrain course of hills, bumps and bridle paths that belonged to Grafham Water on the outskirts of Cambridgeshire. My logistical planning really came up for debate at that point. Having 2 such challenging routes back to back, so late into the 10 days, was a questionable decision and I certainly paid for it. We were welcomed at Grafham Water by yet more keen cheerleaders, wanting to contribute their supporting miles to the cause. I was, of course, delighted to see everyone and was well-practised at putting on a bubbly facade to convince everyone I was perfectly fine, when deep down inside, I was actually mildly terrified because I was pretty sure the next 5 hours or so were going to be rather physically unpleasant. I had a responsibility to this incredible cause and I set off on day 9 with nothing but belief in my psychological resilience to continue to overcome the growing obstacles being placed in front of me.

I think I managed to get to mile 3 relatively pain-free. Jolly good, that meant only the following 23.2 miles to get through with a direct shooting pain gleefully filling most of my left shin. The first lap actually seemed to fly by; you can soon chase down 9 miles when you are distracted by more glorious scenery and a few downhill bursts to look forward to. Despite being in quite considerable pain, I couldn't ignore the fantastic surroundings we were in and the avid support getting us round. I just kept telling myself,

'It's ok if you have to be injured for the next 3 months, Laura. We will deal with any injury after tomorrow. Just get through the next 2 days and you can sit on your arse for a year if you need to.'

I had decided that whatever was going on in my leg, I was still able to put one foot in front of the other without it falling off, so I could probably muddle through it. On the final stretch of lap 2, whilst running parallel to the reservoir, we encountered the biggest swarm of thunder flies I'd ever seen. My fluorescent green top didn't really act as the deterrent I needed but we took the opportunity to devour some extra protein and I ran straight through it open-mouthed like a bloody bush tucker trial. By the end of the half-mile stretch, my shins resembled the neglected front grill of an old car, absolutely smothered in dead black flies. My legs and arms looked like they had developed some sort of skin condition as they were mottled black with dead flies everywhere. I was immensely proud of the fact that even though I was moving so slowly, I was still going fast enough to squash the flies with my heavy little legs. I stopped at mile 18 after completing 2 laps and couldn't quite get my head round running a third. I felt like a formula one driver coming into a pit stop. I just stood there as one pit crew wiped down my fly-speckled arms and legs, another pit crew liberally applied Vaseline to my chafed back and chest, one more was feeding me baby food and water, whilst the final minion was spraying sun cream on any spare surface area of my body. My good friend Lucy tried to massage out some of the crap that had built up in my left shin (I think that probably resembled changing my flat tyre – to maintain the rather farfetched formula one analogy). But I think I was developing something of a slow puncture; my left shin was screaming, even at the softest touch. I was temporarily inflated and patched up and started to attack the last 8 miles of day 9.

I'm still not entirely sure how I made it round those last 8 miles. I think the decision to abandon a full lap of the reservoir and literally run 4 miles out and 4 miles back helped psychologically. The distance would have been the same, but for some reason, this way was easier to break down. I usually look for and take the most difficult path, because they often lead to the most worthwhile locations. But I had no time or patience for philosophical shit at that point. I needed the last 8 miles to be as easy as they could be so I could get them done and rest. Inevitably, the last miles still included hills and a few more of those blasted flies, but I had never experienced such a feeling of relief when I crossed that finish line. I was handed a celebratory Calippo (they were becoming quite a firm favourite) and near enough collapsed on the floor. The pain in my leg was instantly relieved as I lay down and began the search for some sort of pain relief. I strapped an ice pack to my leg secured with an old t-shirt and necked some ibuprofen there and then. I wanted more than anything to be effortlessly embracing this incredible moment, celebrating at the thought of being just one more marathon away from achieving what had been my sole purpose for nearly a year. Even thinking about running another mile at that point was ruining my fragile brain, so I carefully crawled into the car and took that evening an hour at a time.

The evening of day 9 was spent clambering in and out of an ice bath, in between sitting in compression boots on the highest setting, whilst periodically taking pain killers crushed into protein shakes, at the same time as resting as much as possible, as well as massaging my other aches and pains, all whilst trying to eat my bodyweight in pasta. It was like my normal recovery process on steroids, all in a great attempt to ensure marathon 10 was just that – a marathon. I did not want to bow out on a bloody 8-hour romp around my home town. I absolutely refused to walk my last marathon. I was going to run it or at least jog it, even if it meant chopping my throbbing left leg off and hopping round with the 85% or so I have left on my right one.

The morning of day 10 was much the same as the evening of day 9, doing everything conceivable to ensure my body would make it through the final 26.2 miles. I felt anything but fresh and ready to go, but the group of enthusiastic runners congregating at 9am on a drizzly Sunday morning soon bucked my ideas up. The large picture windows of my lounge looked out directly onto the start line of marathon 10 and I couldn't help but feel a sense of pride at the individuals going out of their way to plod alongside me for the first few miles. I shifted the rickety old windows up and let out an awakening,

'GOOOOOD MORNNNINGGG, CAMPERS!!'

Everyone smiled, looked up and waved. I had to grasp every single minute of this last day with both hands and do my very best to put to the back of my mind the pain I was still in. Yet again, a couple of the cheerful crowd gathering on the high street of my home town were complete strangers; complete strangers who had come out to run a marathon with me. One of those strangers was a fascinating gentleman called Bruce. He was a qualified psychologist and a national level runner who had chosen to run one of his monthly training marathons with me. We shared so many of the same views and opinions around the joy that is recreational and competitive running and exercise and soon cemented our friendship within the first few minutes of meeting one another. I forewarned all the athletic individuals surrounding me at the start line,

'This may well be the slowest few miles you'll ever run, folks! I'm a little bit wobbly!'

What that actually translated to was,

'Lads, let's be honest, I'm completely fucked. You'll do well to get a 5k out of me today, never mind a marathon. If I want to walk, I'll walk. If I want to cry, I'll cry and if I ask you for any form of pain relief within the first 5 minutes of meeting you, please administer it to me in any way you can. Thanks.'

Even at that stage of the challenge, I was still concerned at the embarrassment of running slightly slower than I'm used to, or was expected to. I still hadn't acknowledged at all that I had covered 235.8 miles in the last 9 days. I was rather more concerned with convincing people I'd never usually run at this snail's pace, it must be something to do with the 9 consecutive marathons I'd already run. Of course, everyone (apart from me) was more than understanding of my disposition and would have been just as proud and forthcoming had I had to bloody skateboard around the last one. The final marathon consisted of one lap of 8 miles and three laps of 6 miles around my lovely home town of St Ives, every lap allowing for a pit stop directly outside my front door and culminating in the most incredible finish on St Ives Bridge – if we could make it there. The first lap was kind to me and the unbelievable concoction of pills rattling around in my stomach appeared to be doing their job. I'd spent the last 10 days greatly improving my mental maths as I'd sometimes pass the time working out how many more miles I had to run. After around an hour on day 1, I still had 256 miles to cover. After a morning's work on day 4, I still had 173.6 miles to run. So, on that final morning, when I stopped for a baby food sachet and a mouthful of peanuts, the knowledge I had 18 miles left to run was both astonishing and quite unbelievable.18 miles, is that it?! I might just finish this thing. This was a more than appropriate moment to crack out a stalwart, favourite quote of mine to settle the absolute mayhem of my mind,

'Laura - you've not come this far to have only come this far.'

Crunching the numbers gave me an unexpected boost as I was gradually working towards the vision of crossing that bridge and getting entirely inebriated with my closest friends and family, but there was still a way to go yet. I couldn't have been far away from overdosing with the amount of paracetamol flowing round my system, but I just had to accept the pain and keep working through it. As each lap came round, there was more and more of a gathering on the beautiful bridge outside my home. I was running around St Ives with a dedicated following of bikes, runners and walkers. I was also being greeted every 6 miles with well-wishers, patiently waiting at the foot of the bridge for the big finish I was feeling more and more pressured to provide. I couldn't work out whether the majority of the gathering was Sunday afternoon sun-revellers, moseying around feeding the ducks, or whether they were part of my loyal support troop. Either way, anyone not associated with the 10-10-10 take over in St Ives that day was soon to be infiltrated by it if they hung around the finish line much longer!

Any single change in incline in that last 6 miles caused complete agony. Stepping up a kerb, going down a hill, going up a hill, stopping for a drink, waiting for a car, I couldn't mask the pain I was in any more. I was shrieking at any slight movement that wasn't straight, flat or slow. But the physical pain was being very well counter-balanced by the emotional euphoria of being just miles away from the finish I'd been fantasising about for months. The last few miles were slow but jubilant. The usual tracks that I run alone on a weekly basis were illuminated with a community of runners and cyclists that had accompanied me for the last 10 days, 10 miles or 10 minutes (it really didn't matter). We were all joining in with the 'running banter' that (obviously) I was instigating and we were bouncing off one another in one of the most incredible few miles of my life. I think it was only as the faithful watch face struck 25.9 miles that I knew I'd done it. I could have been attacked by an escaped wild grizzly bear and still been ecstatic enough to crawl the last 400 metres to the finish. I could hear the finish before I could see it which was a bloody amazing sign in itself. The approach to the bridge is a long straight road with minimal traffic, so we were literally running 8 abreast, taking up every section of tarmac in the most carefree fashion. There could have been a trail of traffic 20 cars long, but we were not stopping or moving for anyone. Even 100 yards before the finish, which had been expertly crafted out of fresh white toilet roll, there were people lining the bridge, clapping and holding laminated pictures, messages and signs. The noise coming from that small collection of people was superb and as soon as I stepped on the bridge for that last 30 metres, I couldn't hold back the tears any more. I tried to take in what was happening and enjoy the finish to this epic challenge in every way I could. But I was totally overwhelmed by every emotion possible. Relief, euphoria, excitement, pride, exhaustion, disbelief, utter amazement, shock and the purest sense of happiness pulsed through my empty veins. I threw the glorious string of toilet roll high in the air whilst gold confetti cannons exploded around us and I'm sure my smile must have nearly broken my face. I was engulfed in the deafening sound of raucous applause and whooping and as soon as I'd crossed the finish line, I immediately walked back over it again and embraced Amanda in the most emotionally fuelled hug we had ever had. We were both sobbing as she whispered in my ear,

'You've done it, baby. You've done it.'

Friends and family continued to applaud as I sank my head into my hands and cried and cried. I don't think there was a dry eye on the bridge, if I'm honest; as I glanced up, some of my closest friends were also dabbing their slightly blurry eyelids. For probably the first time in my life, I didn't know what to say, where to look or what to do. I was ecstatic but entirely emotionally overwhelmed.

"I shouldn't even be here."

I kept saying that line to myself over and over in my head. I shouldn't even be able to walk. I'm lucky I was even left with a fully functioning leg and there I was, sobbing at the finish line of 10 marathons in 10 days. My own self imagined and planned little baby that I'd just nurtured for the past 9 months had been completed.

I had bloody done it. 262 miles. 10 marathons in 10 consecutive days. Over 48 hours of running over 10 days. 27 energy gels. 18 sachets of baby food. 312 salt and vinegar crisps. 2 gallons of milkshake. 10 ice baths. Pints and pints of Lucozade. A year's supply of Vaseline. 4 packs of blister plasters. £7,080 donated to an incredible charity and countless numbers of lives touched over a week and a half. The biggest physical endurance challenge I'd ever taken on had changed my life immeasurably. I composed myself just enough to make one final finish-line speech where I expressed my unbelievable gratitude for every single gesture, no matter how small, that had contributed to this life-changing experience. I put a great emphasis on the community this venture had created and the brilliantly committed people who had held my hand along the way. I covered myself in the most picture-perfect pink champagne in a celebratory spray, centre stage of St Ives Bridge. I don't care how much of a stereotypical fairy tale ending it all sounded; it was the truth. My whole world, in that moment, was entirely perfect. The vision and ambition that had completely consumed me for the best part of a year were being realised in that very moment. In a similar vain to the sentiment of, 'Don't meet your heroes', the realisation of a dream coming true is near impossible to react to, let alone be able to articulate in black and white. I genuinely had no idea what to do with myself, so, I did what I'd been doing for the last 10 days and totally ignored what my body was telling me to do (find something flat and comfortable to sit on) and instead, stood with my head in my hands and sobbed uncontrollably. The ending just continued to escalate as I was showered with gifts. Flowers, copious amounts of alcohol, cakes, photos, medal-holders – it was like a baby shower for my marathon baby. I'd given life to 10 little marathons and everyone was celebrating, I was probably quite dehydrated and delirious when having that notion too, but who cares. I haven't experienced childbirth but I'm quite sure the pain I was in for that final marathon couldn't have been far off. We all mingled around the bridge sipping Prosecco, pulling little gold rectangles out of our hair from the finish-line confetti cannons, eating copious amounts of cake and all just sat in a moment of rather loud reflection, reminiscing about the most unbelievable 10 days.

The months following 10-10-10 were a brilliant conveyor belt of attention, publicity and heart-warming recognition and compliments from, often, complete strangers. I was in the local news both in print and on the big screen, I spoke on numerous radio stations and ZOOM meetings and for all of the coverage I received, the biggest aspect they were interested in, quite fascinatingly, was the physical state of my body. None chose to pursue the line of questioning about my now invincible psychological health that had been going from strength to strength throughout the 10-day period. They (the infamous media) can't get enough of you when your brain gets the shits and you are left dancing round the A14 hoping for a fatal strike. They are less interested when you have just experienced the most psychologically uplifting 10 days of your life and are totally empowered by your psychological resilience. I reiterate, we are typically very sadistic as a nation, really. We usually thrive off hearing others' trauma, intrigued by the harrowing back story of the next poor sod to flash on the middle page column of a tabloid. But it appeared I was impacting on that norm, if only temporarily. I was turning one of those middle-page horror stories into the sort of positivity, achievement and success you wouldn't have associated with a story like mine in a million years. Well, I took 10 years, but even so, my horror story was screwed up, shredded, thrown in the bin and rewritten in the most life-affirming turn around you'll see for a long time. Social media was flooded with pictures of me from loyal friends and supporters. The reach and capacity of social media are really clear to see when you are literally slathered all over it. The country's media had been ridiculed by Covid-19-induced negativity for the days and weeks leading up to the challenge and to influence that repetitive pattern, if only for a few days, was so moving.

My body, for the vast majority who couldn't get enough of how physically damaged I *must* have been and bearing in mind what it had just been through, was holding up relatively well. The obvious blisters, chafing and fatigue-induced injuries healed relatively smoothly. I did, however, do some quite significant nerve damage to my left shin and foot, leaving the top of my left foot completely numb for months following the end of the challenge. The gasps of my friends and family on the bridge when revealing the significant swelling on my shin were not so reassuring at the time. Even the gentle elastic circumference of the top of my sports sock had left an indented train track circle around my shin and calf, cutting through the very obvious swelling. I visited my trusty physiotherapist on numerous occasions in the months following the challenge and frustratingly, there really isn't much treatment for nerve damage other than rest, specific stretching and some deep tissue work to relieve some of the lingering swelling. Having said that, if you can find me one runner, tri-athlete or athlete of any description in this hemisphere who enjoys doing so much as one thing off this list, never mind all three, I'd run my next marathon backwards, in flip flops. I suppose that is the damage to be expected after running 2 consecutive marathons on an injury that should have been immediately rested for 2-3 weeks. The numbness almost depicted a weird sort of battle scar, though. I was proud that I had some sort of long-term damage as it was a physical representation of what my body had gone through. It could have done the noble thing by hanging around for a week so I could milk it and then bugger off when I wanted to get back to running again, but the nerve damage made itself very comfortable in my foot for months on end. For the very region of my body that had been causing me quite agonising pain for days 9 and 10 of the challenge, to then suddenly turn numb for a few months was worrying, but fantastically ironic at the same time.

I was invited to speak to Scout groups, various school year's assemblies and was even invited to be a guest speaker at the East Anglian Air Ambulance Staff annual gathering. The event was held at the very prestigious Elveden Hall and hosted an array of life-saving people ranging from doctors and paramedics to Heads of Finance for the fundraising department. It was genuinely an honour to be invited and also to be presented with their Inspirational Fundraiser of the Year award. I spoke with the usual gusto I had become accustomed to whilst voicing my mid-run epiphanies over the past month, (that all conveniently happened to be caught on camera) and used it as another practising platform to hone my craft of motivational speaking. I still incur a varying level of shock amongst audiences when I speak quite openly and brashly about walking out in front of a lorry. There is still that annoying unwritten British etiquette of maintaining that stiff upper lip and instead of facing a problem, inconvenience or awkwardness head-on, we quietly ignore it and hope it goes away. I'm very much of the opinion that poor mental health or problems understanding it will never go away, not entirely, and we have to face them head-on, sometimes in the most brutal fashion. I walked out in front of a lorry on the A14, when I was 18, in an attempt to kill myself. No scooting around the facts. Nothing withheld because of the fear of offending someone. No covering up the facts because it might act as a 'trigger' for someone else who is suffering. 'Trigger' is a pathetic, responsibility-shifting and entitled word. If what I have said in an attempt to inspire and educate, has encouraged another person to be triggered into doing something dangerous or of great risk to life, it would not be my responsibility. It would be their external foundations, poorly organised life experiences and incorrect belief systems. It would further be due to an unfortunate lack of knowledge or education and a lack of desire, need or ability to apply themselves properly to obtaining the correct form of psychological help, not because something they heard triggered them. And, if they took the decision upon themselves to do that, then they also take the lion's share of responsibility as well. Walking in front of a lorry is just as much a part of my life and success as running 10 marathons is. The world and his wife want in on the action when you are talking about a charity adventure spanning 262 miles, but they squirm and get mildly uncomfortable when you briefly take them along the path that got you there. In my opinion, the gleaming success at the end is far more genuine and heartfelt if you know the treacherous path many have often taken to get there.

Friends and family carry a horrific burden for the rest of their existence when a loved one takes their own life, viciously questioning whether they could have or should have done more, deeply analysing final phone calls, text messages or social media posts and criticising whether they could have picked up on something or contributed something different to the conversation. Lives are often irreversibly changed after a suicide anyway but what can't happen (yet so often does) is the continuous ripple effect of suicide, the tide taking under everyone and anyone that was within touching distance of that one person and filling them with an unmanageable guilt and so many heart-breaking unanswered questions that inevitably become too much to cope with. The very lost individuals that are left behind by suicide simply cannot adopt and take on the affliction their loved one was carrying with them too. That loved one had a responsibility to themselves and their family to address the dangerous place they were in and owed it to the ones around them to do something about it. I know, I'm preaching again. But I'm warranted in this department to try and provide some comfort to those left behind. My story is one not only of survival and inspiration, but also progression, growth, hard work, responsibility and above all else, education. The more people we can motivate to educate themselves around the best care for their own psychology, the more we can encourage the notion in people that they are enough, and they are worthy of the dedication it takes to improve, the fewer train drivers we are going to be paying off early because they've ploughed into three suicidal souls in the past 6 months. Whatever position you are in reading this (and I genuinely hope it is a healthy psychologically solid one), remember, YOU ARE ENOUGH. You don't have to battle for 10 years and run 10 marathons to realise this like I did. You don't have to run one mile to realise this. Know it here and now. Chief executive, doctor, scientist, cleaner, baker candlestick maker – you are, and always will be, enough.

Chapter 10.

When You've Come So Close to Death –
Every Day Is a Bonus

First and foremost, I don't believe I can fix people –I believe people can fix themselves. I am not trying to imitate a highly qualified psychological professional, preaching to the masses about the most fruitful, successful and positive way to exist. I'm a 27-year-old individual who has had more life experience than I probably should have done and I feel a responsibility to utilise that. What is the point in experiencing so many aspects of life, including all of its inevitable traumatic patches, and not sharing what you have learnt? The reason we progress as a human race is through suffering, learning and ultimately, survival of the fittest, both mentally and physically. I would suggest that it is unfortunate that particular lives have to be sacrificed in order for the world to learn or that numerous people have to suffer in order for progression to happen, but in reality, that is just life. What is very fortuitous, in my opinion, is to have actually experienced a unique life-threatening moment (or more than one) and managed to come out of the other side of it, and as a result, have had the opportunity to develop a renewed appreciation and zest for life. Generally, if life-threatening moments go the way they more than likely should, you don't get the option to discuss it, dissect it or direct the lessons learned towards anyone who might benefit. The very fact that I've survived intentionally walking out in front of a lorry (as well as a minor case of international appendicitis) is a huge blessing and I'm in no way religious. Those two quite irrefutable negatives are two of the best things that happened to me – or rather - two of the best things I have ever done. They have contributed so much to who I am and what I believe in.

Every single slightly important moment life throws up is now even more important. Every single seemingly insignificant joy is never insignificant. When the washing up liquid blows bubbles out when you squeeze it, when you wake up at 5am thinking it's Monday and it turns out to be Sunday and you snuggle back down, when you sink into a hot bath after a long cold run, when your Yorkshire puddings rise perfectly, when you smile every time you spell 'NECESSARY' correctly because you remember your Granddads' acronym, "Never eat cake, eat salad sandwiches and remain young!", when you find a forgotten fiver in your old jeans, your favourite song unexpectedly plays on the radio, you knock over something fragile and catch it just at the right moment, you find the end of the Sellotape first time, you bite into a KitKat and there is no wafer, you take the first mouthful of your favourite dinner after thinking about it all day, when you get caught in the rain whilst running and feel so free, so alive, so invincible. All of those ridiculous little life moments are all so much more significant now, because at one point in my life, there was a really strong chance I would have never been able to do or see or feel any of them again.

I think a huge problem we have in our culture is that too many people spend their life completely focussed on the desire to escape discomfort. I've found if you actually strive to do the opposite, your life and appreciating what a privilege it is becomes so much easier. So, below are 10 (there is definitely some sort of numerical theme here...) of some of the biggest life lessons I live by and still learn from every day. If even just one human being benefits from the small philosophies I employ on a daily basis, if they progress or enhance their life by reading something I've written in this book, well, mission accomplished.

If you've already seen the bottom then there is nothing to fear.

Every single person has one. Just like the ghost stories you shared at teenage sleepovers or one of those stomach-churning embarrassing stories where you sent an explicit text to your boss, everyone also has their own horror story. A recollection of an event, incident or time frame, which, if told in person, would leave most people in tears. Everybody has their 'rock bottom', their own personal abyss where they deemed their life simply couldn't get any worse. This is the first and most important lesson I live by and my 'rock bottom' was back in my old Bed and Breakfast, Addenbrooke's Hospital. I'd just returned from one of the surgeries on my leg and was recovering in substantial pain on the ward. My infectious 'Clostridium-Difficile' was just revving up and my bowels were dispensing downwards just as quickly as my stomach was shooting upwards. My right arm was suffering from incessant cramping due to two severe wounds affecting the nerve endings in my forearm. I had lost any control I had over my mental state and I was just a bed-bound firework display of negative emotions coming to terms with what I had done. I actually made one of the nurses cry as I pleaded with her for her help. I begged her to take some of the pain away. I essentially begged her to put me out of my misery. The one positive thought that I clung on to for every single minute of that incredibly dark night was,

"IT CANNOT GET ANY WORSE THAN THIS."

I lay there that night, alone, my body often contorted with pain, repeating it in my head,

"There is nothing I will face in my life now that can be any worse than this."

Any form of mental and physical suffering will pale in to complete insignificance compared to that night. Anything that life should throw at me, from that night forward, I'll catch it one-handed and throw it right back. That night taught me the greatest lesson in perspective that I have ever had. The solid understanding of perspective I have developed throughout the past 10 years originated on that night. That night was my abyss. I have no fear of suffering or discomfort now, because nothing will come close to that night. I have no fear of failure now because that night, I felt like you could open the Oxford Dictionary and the definition of failure would have a picture of me just slumped there. But I damn well made it through that night and made it to the next morning so I could start to build back up again. Whenever my life has a little stumble, I purposefully remind myself of that night, take a step back and question whether what I am dealing with is really that bad. I usually confirm it is nothing that can't be solved with a bit of time, a bit of effort or a bit of sacrifice. Figure out what your 'bottom' is or was and congratulate yourself when you realise just how far up you have worked since being there. Then you can forever use it as a reference point to determine whether you need to take time to work through a rough patch or, very simply, just get a grip.

Success in anything is a result of continuous and persistent effort. "A stone is broken by the last stroke of the hammer; that doesn't mean the first stroke is useless."

This is applicable to so much in life, not just in mine but in yours as well. Everyday won't be a brilliant day; that is pretty well established. Some days you'll wake up at 6am, skip out of the front door and be at hot pod yoga by 6:15. You'll have a kale smoothie for breakfast, steam through your working day without a glitch, come home and smash out a 5k, make a superfood salad for dinner and pack your kids healthy lunches in colour co-ordinated Tupperware for the next 4 days. You'll educate yourself on global topical issues with the 10pm headlines before getting an early night on your freshly washed and ironed bedspread. Other days, you'll fall out of bed, have a bowl of out-of-date Frosties, vegetate in your unwashed, old pyjamas in front of Netflix for 8 hours and then crawl back into your pit. And that is just fine. There is no need to be self-deprecating on those days. Some days, throughout the very cathartic and rewarding process of writing this book, I'd plough through 2,000 words in a morning and feel like everyone of them was articulate, relevant and detailed. Other days, I'd write 100 words, then delete 200, then mix 'their' up with 'there' and mistake 'your' for you're', put a comma where there should have been a semicolon and come to the conclusion I might be better illustrating a dot-dot picture book. Whatever level of success you achieve in your day, you've still made it through, haven't you? Even in the very darkest of days, there will be a tiny morsel of progress you can cling to. Those 8-hour long Netflix binge days? They were full of rest and recuperation. That is not lazy or unproductive, it is progressive self-care. Let's say the average life expectancy nowadays is 80 years. There are 365 days in a year. If you live to be 80, that is a total of 29,200 days you have lived through. Jesus Christ. Even if you have 100 bad days a year (2 a week), that still gives you such an abundance of time to rectify that. When you do come through the good, the bad and the ugly and you finally break your stone, remember that on those days when you were whacking and whacking and thinking you weren't even making a dent, you actually were, more than you know!

Everything will be ok in the end. If it's not ok, it's not the end.

This may initially seem contradictory to the whole approach to the book. It might appear that this philosophy advocates just waiting it out, letting the world pass you by and not being pro-active in taking responsibility to help yourself or your circumstances. On the contrary, I believe this approach is about tolerance and understanding of the situation you are in. When you are at the start of a 12-hour shift, you're tired, dejected and nothing feels ok. It feels as though you are at the bottom of a sizeable hill with not even a slab of Kendal mint cake to help you to the top. But you slowly begin to tolerate those temporary negative feelings and gradually start taking steps up the hill and through your day, like you have done so many times before. You enjoy the momentary peaks of the day where you are able to pause and take in the view. But you also endure the troughs where you simply need to get your head down, plough on and accept that you will navigate every obstacle in your path until you reach the top of your hill. Tolerance is the self-belief and ability to accept the adverse conditions you may be facing and continue on, regardless of your physical discomfort or psychological doubt. It is about understanding that, occasionally, those conditions will actually worsen before you obtain your goal but the hardship will only ultimately make your victory sweeter. The more adversity you face upon your journey, the greater your tolerance becomes. When you do finally make it to the top of your own personal hill, in whatever scenario you apply this metaphor to, make sure you grab that finish with both hands and use it for the incredibly valuable life lesson that it is. Then, the next time you are at the start line of a 12-hour shift, a long weekend with the in-laws, an operation, an important interview, a list of housework as long as your arm, a work presentation, a disciplinary process, a marathon, just remember the physical and psychological tolerance you built up in your last battle before this one. You can then rely upon it and build upon it to carry you over the next set of hurdles which the day, week or just life may place in front of you.

"If you can take the sourest lemon life has to offer and turn it into something resembling lemonade, then, how much you sell is actually irrelevant."

I've developed a small, local reputation over the last few months of being the 'marathon woman' due to running 262 miles in 10 days. Not sure if I've already mentioned it?? I'm quite moved and proud of the nickname that has been bestowed upon me. But despite that accolade and the achievements behind it, I still celebrate every single 5k that I run because every run is still so meaningful, regardless of the distances you have reached before. It is so easy for the people you surround yourself with to start wearing away at your self-confidence with comments regarding your previous achievements. I'm sure many of you can relate to the conversation, more often than not said in jest, that begins,

'But you've already run a marathon; this should be easy for you!!'

Now, whilst I'm the biggest advocate for building on your achievements and pushing the boat out just that little bit further every time, that in no way means I don't also believe in celebrating every single small victory in the journey to greater things. I don't care if you have run 1,000 marathons in 1,000 days. Running 26.2 miles is, and always will be, an epic feat of human endurance and it should be acknowledged, rewarded and celebrated no matter how experienced you are.

Olympic athletes literally run hundreds of 10k, 5k or 800-metre distances every single week in training. But when it comes to the actual event, being held in an erupting amphitheatre of pressure, tension and expectation, you don't whisper over their shoulder,

'Pah, you'll be fine; you've done this so many times before!'

Even though that's probably an appropriate attitude to soften the nerves of any well-trained athlete, it is not the point. The point is that practice and dedication are what made them so successful in the first place. All of their training should be celebrated, alongside the final victory. The 10k they ran in training is no less significant than the Olympic Final, because it was those 5am lonely training runs that got them to the final in the first place.

You don't continue to achieve distances you've already completed with the goal to go slower, or because you don't fancy going the extra miles. You continue to achieve when you are running, full stop. The motivation to get out of your front door some days needs to be so great that your usual Wednesday night 5k may as well have been an Olympic event. So, when life does smack you in the face with those 'sour lemons' of significant life events, uncontrollable pandemics or illness, lack of sleep or any other form of stress, should you get so much as one glass of lemonade out of it, you be damn well proud of that glass and celebrate your small victory or your 'small' run. If you get through those aforementioned inconveniences and still come out with something resembling lemonade, you take that glass, however small, and enjoy every sip. Some days are filled with monumental victories that you'll remember for the rest of your life. Other days, your biggest victory is doing the washing up before you go to bed so you don't have to face it in the morning. Sometimes a compilation of the seemingly small victories, that no one else around you ever notices other than yourself, lead to the big ones we are allowed to shout about even louder.

A woman's reach should exceed her grasp.

This is another absolute corker of a line that can be entirely accredited to Sir Robert Browning as it is derived from his poem, 'Andrea Del Sarto.' The entire quote is actually,

'Ah, but a man's reach should exceed his grasp, or what's a heaven for!'

Obviously, that meant I had to adapt it slightly to include a female pronoun at the start but the gender referred to is irrelevant. Browning here perfectly encapsulates the never-ending pursuit of bettering oneself and reaping the positive progress associated with it. This, to me, is a far more eloquent expression of,

'Do something that scares you.'

Browning alludes to the fact that achieving something you thought was beyond your capabilities is satisfyingly pleasant with a reference to heaven, suggesting that when you obtain your impossible goal, your ticket to the pearly gates is all but confirmed. I couldn't agree more with his attitude of essentially,

'Always bite off more than you can chew.'

Therefore, you can see if you are actually able to chew it right up and spit it out. How else do we ascertain whether something actually is impossible? There was a time, not so long ago, when running a sub-10-second 100 metres was 'impossible', running a sub-2-hour marathon was 'impossible', reaching the peak of Everest was 'impossible', a female serving in ALL front-line military roles was impossible. All modern history trailblazers have done is changed what they believed was possible, worked unbelievably hard and been brave enough to chase their runaway ambition. So why can't we apply that mindset to our everyday normality? Maybe what appears to be beyond our grasp actually isn't and it just takes some courage and determination to succeed? It is an innate human characteristic to avoid sources of fear or circumstances we know are going to produce uncertainty. Therefore, it is natural to remain where we are safe and comfortable, but no progress is ever made there. Comfort is the enemy of progress. If we could just allow ourselves to be immersed in discomfort and unpredictability for a short time to see what we can actually achieve, the potential of the human race would explode. I'm forever seeking the next adventure that is going to push my boundaries just that little bit further. It will always be something I think that I can't do, so that if and when I do complete it, that self-confidence, belief and powerful independence continues to mature.

This particular lesson sang loudest to me throughout the book-writing process, actually. I'd received the inevitable lack of belief from a number of people that I actually thought I wouldn't. You tell a small handful of acquaintances that you are writing a book, and, because they have never followed that process themselves, they passively dismiss it as yet another pipe dream that won't ever really come to fruition. Funnily enough, I've never written a book before this one, so this particular ambition was arguably well beyond my grasp. People are far more accepting of something you are trying to achieve if it resonates with them personally, they have some experience of it or they can relate to it. Or most importantly, they've actually seen it done. The typical reaction to, 'I'm writing a book', is a polite smile and patronising nod with an undertone of, 'Well, I'll believe that when I see it.'

What most people don't understand is that literary success is not reserved for the J.K Rowlings, Stephen Kings or other fantastic authors of the world. It is actually sat there waiting for anyone who has the guts to go after it (a decent story or idea helps along the way too, obviously). The majority of people don't like it when you say you are doing something that is so far beyond their own personal realms of potential, because it makes them feel less worthy or threatened in some way. Proudly project the idea you are going on a diet, getting a puppy or having a baby and people are more than comfortable with that as they perceive it as something they themselves could probably attain with a small amount of effort. It doesn't threaten their own personal opinion of themselves. Explain you are writing a book or running an ultra-marathon or swimming the channel, and most will either just politely dismiss it to ensure it doesn't damage their pride in some way, or insult it in jest, again not meaning to hurt your feelings but to protect themselves from their own self-created insecurity. Your own personal path of self-betterment and achievement becomes threatening and envy-inducing to a small minority, so they distance themselves from it for their own protection. I reach beyond my grasp in so many areas of my life, not to threaten or compete with others, but because it fulfils me in a way that nothing else I've found so far in life can compete with.

People often get it disastrously wrong when they set themselves a challenge in life, whether it is physically or psychologically based. This is not through not trying, but because the idea of a challenge is interpreted incorrectly. Challenging yourself isn't about finding something you hate then going out and doing it repetitively, for however many torturous days or weeks, to prove you have accomplished something. Nor is it about depriving yourself of something you love, again for those torturous days and weeks so you can celebrate your new-found self-discipline and willpower. If that thing you love is a detriment to your health then giving it up is more of a necessity than a self-constructed, life-affirming challenge. If you love chocolate but have found yourself smashing 6 Freddos a day, then maybe start setting some limitations to say, one a day, for example. Start weaning yourself off it. Giving up something for the benefit of your health is not a life-affirming challenge or memorable reference point – it is a necessary improvement that needs to be taken under control. The challenge for a chocolate lover would not be to start depriving yourself of it, but to perhaps start monitoring your intake a bit better, and then educate yourself, work a bit of overtime, research and learn how to be a chocolatier. Imagine the sense of fulfilment making your own designer chocolate bar would bring – if that was what you loved to do. Setting challenges is about exactly that, the level of fulfilment it will give you and reaching the fantastic potential you haven't come close to before. Yes, depriving yourself of something can be physically and mentally tough, but what tangible reward do you get at the end? It is exactly the same as if you hate running but sign up to do a 10k. Yes, I'm sure the finish line feeling will provide the same ecstasy as all finish lines do, but other than the fortunate few that fall in love with something they previously despised, you'll cross the finish line and never run another step because you really resented all the training you had to do. If you loved walking and applied yourself to a walking challenge, you'd cross the finish line, experience the same elation, but because you loved it so much, you would go above and beyond next time. Completing the challenge itself presents another open door, you've already closed the previous one because you reached what you thought was your full potential. But potential will forever be a game of cat and mouse. You reach what you thought was your ultimate potential, but because you successfully reached it, you know you can push a little bit further next time. Always pursue what you love and know your potential is limitless.

You drown not by falling into the river, but by being submerged by it.

As soon as a negative event occurs in life, it is a very normal (but not necessarily beneficial) reaction to become entirely and wholly pessimistic and allow that one event to impact on all the other previously unaffected areas of your life. If you allow it, you become totally governed by whatever has happened and your life and your decisions no longer are your own. You become 'submerged' by it, panic and completely lose the ability to create rational thoughts and decisions that you would have made with ease beforehand. All of a sudden, one event that has inevitably happened through no fault or contribution of your own has taken your composed and controlled demeanour and flipped it on its arse.

Exactly like the reaction when you actually fall into cold water, the best thing to do is remain calm, breathe, tolerate the huge discomfort of freezing water and work out what to do within your control to improve the situation you are in. Instead, chuck most people in a freezing lake and they will flap, splutter, become totally overwhelmed and swallow a stomach full of stagnant water before probably regurgitating it. It wasn't the falling in that caused that reaction, it was themselves. So, whatever it is that negatively impacts on your life, you have to ask yourself, is it the event causing this level of stress or is it my reaction to it? Some of the biggest causes of significant life events are totally beyond your control. You can't control death, you can't control illness, you can't control whether your spouse can keep it in their pants, and you can't control other people's actions. The only thing you can control is how you react to them. Let everyone else splash around like a drunken octopus when life dunks them in an unexpected muddy puddle. You take your time and accept the temporary discomfort, have confidence in your ability to deal with abrupt change, have the belief that this will not last forever and start doing whatever you can to swim to the shore.

This life lesson relates directly to the very well-known phrase in endurance sport -control the controllables. You will not find a successful athlete (or human being for that matter) of any kind that doesn't abide by the mindset of applying yourself unreservedly in the areas you have control over and admirably accepting the areas you don't and adapting to whatever scenario they produce for you. If you can't change your current reality then you need to adapt to it and educate yourself to embrace it and enjoy it. Ross Edgely, the well-known British swimmer and adventurer, uses a memorable quote to sum up this practice;

'Don't fight what you can't beat.'

Your precious energy is entirely wasted fighting against the cold water or poor weather in a vain attempt to change it. You can't change the freezing water. What you can do is equip yourself properly to deal with the conditions with fancy wet suits and neoprene hats and get your body moving again (physically and metaphorically). Your energy is wasted trying to impress your dear mother-in-law (or whatever family member is the thorn in your side) that causes you no end of grief simply because of who you are. Don't fight what you can't beat. Accept that family member for their views, opinions and behaviour, no matter how Neanderthal or inexplicable they are and do not let that impact on your progress. You can't control their reaction to you or your personality that presents no issue to any other of your nearest and dearest. So, allow them to wallow and you carry on being awesome. Your energy is and was wasted worrying about one of the most uncontrollable diseases of our generation – Covid-19. As a worldwide community, we've never experienced such uncertainty and apprehension. But worrying is like sitting on a rocking horse, you can do it all day and it won't get you anywhere. We may well not beat Coronavirus, but fighting against 'it' and its restrictions in any way that isn't medically or scientifically based is counterproductive. We must adapt to the uncontrollable nature of it and channel our energy into positively dealing with it and any other anomalies it throws our way.

The one who falls and gets up is so much stronger than the one who never fell.

It is very easy to be positive and productive when everything is going well and your road has been smooth for a while. It is effortless to radiate enthusiasm and energy when you are doing well and gliding along without a glitch. It becomes a lot harder when you hit that man-size pothole that would derail a bloody tram; only then do you begin to learn something about your resilience. Taking on seemingly insurmountable tasks is a breeze when you haven't encountered failure for a while. You almost become a bit over-confident as you've had nothing memorable to knock you down a few pegs. I often employ another of my favourite sayings when life is flowing well,

'Call me ham and cheese, I'm on a roll!'

But failure is such an important part of success. There is nothing more counterproductive than success becoming straightforward. Success is only valuable when it is properly earned. We should all fail more often and we should expose ourselves to situations where the potential to fail is high because then we appreciate the sacrifice and commitment required to succeed.

The majority of us have a completely incorrect approach to failure; we label it as a negative. But there is a difference between failing and choosing to fail and therefore adopting a self-fulfilling prophecy. If you have already predisposed yourself to fail in a situation because you believe you have no power to succeed in it, that's a personal choice. For example,

'I could never run a marathon; it is too far.'

You instantaneously set yourself up for failure because you have a solid belief you can't achieve something; therefore, you proceed to put no effort into training, and then inevitably fail because you didn't train properly. You then reinforce to yourself that you weren't capable and everyone should have listened to you in the first place, essentially fulfilling the prophecy which you and only you set for yourself at the outset. That is *choosing* to fail. If you have failed when you were given all the assistance and every resource possible to succeed and the failure was due to a lack of belief and effort (because you purposefully wanted your negative belief to be reinforced) – the problem is with your attitude. There is very little positive to come from exposure to that sort of failure. But if you haven't obtained your goal even though you have dedicated every inch of your being to it, you know that all that groundwork will only build an unbreakable foundation for your second attempt. There is a marked difference between failing and choosing to fail: Falling off your bike because you couldn't be arsed to practise because you can't accept your belief system is wrong, or falling off because you were going faster than ever to beat your time are both completely different. Failure fuels the fire of success. The more and more you keep falling off your bike, it shouldn't encourage a belief that you are not good enough to do it. It should heighten the drive to succeed. The more you fail, the more you learn about how to be even better. The more you fail, the more of a holistic human being you become. Failure allows you to respect the commitment needed for success and ensures you never take triumph for granted. Eventually, you will become an expert in the activity that was once shrouded in failure and you can take great satisfaction in attributing your success to your own commitment and perseverance.

Always be kind to everyone that you meet. Remember that flowers bloom when the sun shines; they open up because they trust its warmth. People do too.

In my opinion, the single most important quality that underpins success in any form, in any pursuit, is POSITIVITY. The above quote is taken from talented poet James McInerney and emphatically encourages the infectious nature of positivity. In the same way that wealth breeds wealth, positivity breeds positivity and people unconsciously gravitate towards it. There will always be a positive in every single day, admittedly some days you have to look slightly harder, but committing to finding at least one positive within a 24-hour period can completely transform your outlook. Throughout the Covid-19 pandemic, so many succumbed to the catastrophic picture that was being painted of the world, entirely catalysed by the media. It was so easy to become victimised by what was happening all around us and forget to adopt a positive disposition when it was needed the most. Covid-19 taught us that positivity and happiness are not wrapped up in materialistic objects; genuine contentment is found in the love and company of others and the most basic pleasures we take for granted every day. Happiness is hugging your best friend, it's a game of football with your kids, it's chilling with the family watching a shit film, it's football training, it's a cuppa with your mate, it's running club, it's surrounding yourself with people with exactly the same zest for life as you. When we were temporarily deprived of those things, it made being positive even more simple, because we craved them, so much.

Positivity is a choice and that is what people are drawn to. It is a brave, admirable decision to adopt a positive outlook when you are surrounded by tangible negativity and that is what is attractive to people, not just your positivity itself, but the realisation they could be experiencing the same emotion if they *chose* to. Positivity is hard work in modern-day life but the rewards are so worth the often-draining sacrifice of finding strength and resilience when the washing machine has flooded for the 3rd time this month and payday still seems light-years away. Surround yourself with happy, driven people and the power of positivity will soon seep into you and out of you completely effortlessly.

If you expect the world to be fair with you because you are fair, you are fooling yourself. That's like expecting the lion not to eat you because you didn't eat him.

Sometimes, life will eat you up, swallow you down, spit you out and walk all over you with its size 12 steel cap boots. Then, you give it a few months, recover slightly, get back on your feet and it will do exactly the same thing again. Because that's what life does. It is irrelevant if you give £20 to the donkey sanctuary every month, never break the speed limit and volunteer at the homeless shelter on a Friday night; very often bad things happen to very good people. You can almost guarantee that dodgy Dave down the road steals from the donkey sanctuary charity box in the chippy but will probably win the lottery next week. In the same essence, sometimes very good things happen to bad people. Becoming entitled because you've had your fair share of rough patches is not only incredibly unattractive and senseless but also such a contradiction to the morality and values those life bumps should have taught you. As soon as you come to the realisation that enough exposure to adversity will eventually manifest itself in great resilience and psychological durability, you're almost waiting for the shitter of a day to come flying over the net at you, just so you can return it like Serena. If you start blaming the world for your problems, you lose so much of your independent power to deal with them. If you attempt to start controlling the uncontrollable, you'll just triple your stress levels. Deal with what you can control to the very best of your ability and allow that authority to empower you.

I saw this very piece of advice blatantly ignored over and over again in my time as a Police Officer and it was unbearably frustrating. So many of the young people we would deal with had a very rough start and arguably, didn't know (or hadn't ever seen) any better. However, as you grow and mature, you develop an understanding of the rules of life. Irrespective of whether you had the willingness to abide by them, you know the difference between right and wrong. Yet, the excuse of their terrible past being the reason for their dismal future would rear its ugly head almost daily. Yes, they were undoubtedly failed by an abundance of incomprehensibly incompetent organisations and broken systems to nicely complement their atrocious upbringing. But, (and it's a big but) your shit childhood does not entitle you to become a shit human being, kid. You are not entitled to your own set of rules just because you've had it a bit tougher than most, none of us are. Take responsibility for your past. Keep it stored neatly away in the bits and bobs cupboard, open the door every day and smile at it, knowing it has built you and contributed to who you are as an individual. Don't open that door and let it shit all over you, your actions and your decisions every day. Your past is your responsibility and yours alone and having a torrid start in life makes you entitled to nothing.

With knowledge, comes responsibility.

A very great man told me this piece of advice and I intend to share it with as many people as I can. His name is Rob Kelly and he is the founder of the Thrive Programme. I can attribute a great deal of my psychological resilience to this man and the invaluable lessons he teaches in his book, 'Learn to Thrive.' You must remember that the more you educate yourself and empower yourself, in any subject, including psychological well-being, the more individuals you will come across that will not share your knowledge. If you are choosing to learn more about coping with your mental health, it is your responsibility to try and not only impart your wisdom on others, but also understand that others will have a different outlook to you, possess a different mindset to you, perceive positives and negatives differently to you, and hold potentially restrictive thoughts and unsympathetic principles and morals. But most importantly, they think their way of viewing the world is correct and yours is not. It is a bit like parenting adults.

You know and you understand that every bad day will eventually do you some good, but others may not, so your reactions will be different. You take the approach that when you are in a dark place, maybe you have been planted whereas so many others will think they have been buried. You have a responsibility to those people around you to share your positive knowledge with them and pull them out of the dark with your helping hand. Other people's lack of knowledge can often be met with frustration because they have chosen not to educate themselves and you have. Why should you go through the hardship of completely changing your outlook and challenging what you believe about life to have some freeloader rinse you of all your hard work and commitment? Because you have a responsibility to share your knowledge and understand others may not be as far along their journey as you are. Encourage them to get to a place where they too can use their knowledge for good and take some weight off your workload! But don't be disheartened should some fall by the wayside as you try to educate and liberate. Significant change takes big commitment and that can scare some people. Many are not ready to be scared, you must just be ready for them when they are.

When you finish an endurance challenge of any sort, people react in a similar fashion to how they would when you have just had a kid.

"Ahhh, congratulations! When are you having another one?!"

The expectation is that even though you have just been through a life-changing journey and now have a new baby to cherish and enjoy, you should probably get cracking with the next one to, I don't know, keep up appearances?! When I finished 10-10-10, granted I didn't have a screaming, smelly bundle of joy to financially and emotionally cripple me for the next 20 years, but I had come to the end of a life-changing endeavour. Straight away I was being asked what I would be taking on next as I had now surpassed running 26.2 miles as a worthwhile, personal endurance challenge.

I can no longer use, 'Did you know I'm running a marathon?' as the impressive conversation-starter it once was. I must achieve bigger and better from here on in because that is the very proud precedent I have set. But I must also take the time to cherish all the challenges I have created, planned and executed to fully appreciate them for what they are. Just like a new-born, it must be loved, enjoyed and appreciated before you disrupt it slightly by bringing in a new sibling to knock them off their throne.

However, the philosophies and life lessons I abide by, which I have just outlined, say nothing about sitting around reminiscing on what has been and gone. Rather, each one has an undertone of,

"Get up, get going and jump all over that next opportunity that you have either dug out for yourself or life has graciously given you. Because you are so bloody privileged to even be able to physically (or metaphorically) jump at the opportunity, never mind take it on in all its glory."

There is still an English Channel to swim. There is still a Mount Everest to climb. There is still a Marathon des Sables to run. There is still a North Pole Marathon to run. There is still plenty of 24-hour periods to see how many 'burpees' can be done within them. There is still a good number of Guinness World Records to be broken including 'Fastest Marathon run backwards dressed as a chameleon.' But there are also lazy Sunday mornings to be had where your poached eggs on avocado toast are that perfectly yellow and runny, they just must be posted to Instagram. There are still glorious summer evenings to watch the sun set and wipe the sand in between your toes. There is still getting home after a long day to a warm house and a cooked meal. There is still hearing your kids and grandkids excitedly tell you about their triumphs, their plans and their failures. There is still putting your head on the pillow (even after you have had a shitter of a day) and knowing you have the opportunity to give life another go tomorrow. There is still waking up every day and experiencing the unquestionable privilege of being ALIVE. There will come a time when we are not and we must embrace *all* that life has to offer now because no one else will do it for you. Only you will suffer if you don't. If today were the last day of your life, would you want to do what you are about to do today? If the answer has been 'No' for too many days in a row, you need to change something. Now, then, where did I put that wetsuit...?

Lightning Source UK Ltd.
Milton Keynes UK
UKHW022122070722
405543UK00006B/159